BEACH HOUSES
FROM MALIBU TO LAGUNA

BEACH HOUSES

FROM MALIBU TO LAGUNA

ELIZABETH McMILLIAN

PHOTOGRAPHS BY MELBA LEVICK

FOREWORD BY FRANK GEHRY

RIZZOLI
NEW YORK

Frontispiece: Malibu Pier

First published in the United States of America in 1994 by
RIZZOLI INTERNATIONAL PUBLICATIONS, INC.
300 Park Avenue South, New York, New York 10010

Copyright © 1994 Rizzoli International Publications, Inc.
Text copyright © 1994 Elizabeth McMillian
Photographs copyright © 1994 Melba Levick

Library of Congress Cataloging-in-Publication Data

McMillian, Elizabeth Jean.
Beach Houses from Malibu to Laguna / by Elizabeth McMillian;
photographs by Melba Levick; foreword by Frank Gehry.
p. cm.
ISBN 0-8478-1802-0
1. Seaside architecture—California—Los Angeles Region.
2. Architecture, Domestic—California—Los Angeles Region.
3. Architecture, Modern—20th century—California—
Los Angeles Region.
I. Levick, Melba. II. Title
NA7575.M18 1994
728'.37'0979793—dc20   93-38144
CIP

Designed by Gilda Hannah
Printed in Singapore

CONTENTS

FOREWORD BY FRANK GEHRY   7

FROM MALIBU TO LAGUNA   9

LECHUZA POINT • MALIBU   18
Lynn and Stanley Byer Residence

POINT DUME • MALIBU   28
Annette Smith Residence
David Anawalt Residence
Charles Arnoldi and Katie Anawalt Residence

PARADISE COVE • MALIBU   48
Olivia Newton-John and Matt Lattanzi Residence

MALIBU COLONY BEACH   58
Ilene and Stanley Gold Residence
Dan and Kristi Stevens Residence

MALIBU LAGOON   74
The Rhoda and Merritt Adamson House

CARBON TO LAS TUNAS BEACHES • MALIBU   84
Lisette and Norman Ackerburg Residence
Karen and David Gray Residence

SANTA MONICA BEACH   100
The Louis B. Mayer House
Romy and Neal Israel Residence

VENICE BEACH   114
Lyn and Bill Norton Residence
Carol and Roy Doumani Residence

HERMOSA BEACH • SOUTH BAY   134
Paul and Janice Shank Residence
Andrea Rich Residence

RANCHO PALOS VERDES • PALOS VERDES PENINSULA   142
Katina Torino Residence

NAPLES CANAL • LONG BEACH   152
Ronald and Susan Crowell Residence

BALBOA PENINSULA AND CORONA DEL MAR • NEWPORT BEACH   160
Balboa Peninsula Residence
Joe and Etsuko Price Residence

CRYSTAL COVE • LAGUNA BEACH   178
Martha Padve/Sally and Don Martin Cottage

MOSS POINT • LAGUNA BEACH   186
The Moss Point House
Michael and Linda Hall Residence

SOUTH LAGUNA BEACH   196
South Laguna Point Residence

FOREWORD

When my family and I came to Los Angeles from Toronto in 1947, the beach was the most attractive part of the move. In Canada we had mountains, snow, and ice hockey, but Southern California had the ocean, beaches, and surfing. I was seventeen and impressed by the glamorous and pleasurable life of the beach. More than that, I was taken by the fact that, despite storms, mudslides, and fires, many Californians took risks and dared convention to live near the ocean.

Some years later, I recognized that the beach—the special point where land meets ocean—was a necessary presence in my life. My wife, Berta, is from Panama and is used to being by the water, so naturally we have lived on the coast. Our sons, Alejandro and Sami, have grown up in this expansive environment where they enjoy the water and the view as well as skateboarding, rollerblading, surfing, and the general variety of characters and entertainment found along the boardwalks of Venice and Santa Monica. We'd feel claustrophobic if we lived any further inland. Coming home from any trip, I'm exhilarated to see the glimmering ocean appear as I clear the tunnel where the Santa Monica Freeway meets the water.

The beach inspires dreaming, dreamers, and artists, and it seems to engender the free creative spirit. I felt an affinity to this freedom, and I think I began to truly understand it when I was studying art and architecture in college and later when I started to practice architecture. Many of my artist friends lived and worked in Venice and Santa Monica and I soon joined them. An occasional beach house renovation came my way in those early days; since then I've designed and renovated quite a few, and the programs have varied according to the client's response to the site. With the remodeling of a Malibu Beach house for Jennifer Jones and the late Norton Simon, I began to work with the imagery of angled two-by-fours that appeared to tumble from the roof, capturing some of the process and impermanence natural to the beach setting.

My favorite beach house design was for Bill and Lyn Norton, built during a liberating and unique period in my career. At the time, my office was on the Venice boardwalk and, although Bill and Lyn asked for something simple and tightly budgeted, I took the opportunity to translate elements and images from my daily life creatively. Bill writes and Lyn paints; given their artistic understanding, I worked without constraint to capture the resonance of the location and the neighboring buildings, incorporating the repetitive form of the ever-present lifeguard stations. In the end, the Norton House is appropriate not only to Venice; it also harmonizes with the California beach. In fact, the lifeguard station imagery of the Norton House reminds me of my first idyllic impressions of Los Angeles. The architecture itself represents the concept of California beaches and their defining panoramas.

In this book, Elizabeth McMillian and Melba Levick set out to examine the relationship of house to ocean. Their selection of houses is a sampling of some of the best and most characteristic Southern California designs, demonstrating the ways that residents adapt and decorate their beach homes. Many of my colleagues—architects John Lautner, Richard Meier, Charles Moore, Frank Israel, Ray Kappe, and Bart Prince, and artists Charles Arnoldi and Robert Graham—have contributed their diverse talents to the beach house genre. Their individual styles reveal their attitudes toward beach living and, often, their formal abstractions of natural elements. Yet I find that my own goal is to capture the free-wheeling vitality of the vernacular buildings as well as the beach and boardwalk life that keeps me returning to this extraordinary edge of the world.

Frank Gehry
November, 1993

FROM MALIBU TO LAGUNA

An ocean view is but one reward for those who craft a home on the beach. A beach house can express freedom and attunement with nature, and it is often the fulfillment of a dream as well as a quest for the sensual varieties of site, sound, and touch—the opportunity to feel gentle breezes, warm to the reassuring rays of the sun, and hear the lulling, rhythmic sound of wind and waves.

Beaches and beach houses have played an important part in the historical and cultural development of Southern California. In a number of real estate building booms beginning in the 1880s, developers created seaside resorts to attract investors and home-buyers from colder climates and inland terrain. By the 1920s, the motion picture community and other residents with new wealth built lavish beachside houses and beach clubs, more often for social reasons than for family recreation. Following World War II, California's increased population meant more people frequented the shore at sites placed under the care of the newly-formed Division of Beaches and Parks. The younger generation found that beach life provided both pleasure and an escape from conventional social distinctions associated with urban settings. By the 1960s, some of these adventurous baby boomers made a cult of surfing.

At almost any coastal body of water, beach house owners can swim, sail, fish, snorkel, and sunbathe, but only in Southern California can they surf at the best and most frequented surfing beaches. The sport was introduced in California by George Freet, an Anglo-Hawaiian who brought his large, heavy surfboard from Hawaii to Redondo Beach in 1907 for surfing exhibitions sponsored by Henry E. Huntington as part of a real estate promotion. Surfing became popular in the 1950s and 1960s after Bob Simmons developed a lightweight synthetic board. A number of films, songs, and books in the 1960s fueled the surfing movement and the corresponding stereotype of California life. From quaint to glamorous, beach houses were an essential backdrop to this image of life on Southern California beaches.

Most people who now live along the oceanfront, however, are quite serious about keeping out surfers and the rest of the world, yet bringing in the view. Typically, beach house owners deal with the restrictions of a small lot and have evolved a standard formula that includes a relatively low key and enclosed street facade; enclosed sidewalls; narrow paths that run the length of the lot from the street to the beach, and a glass-walled or terraced oceanfront. Within these parameters, each house can be either unique or commonplace, a waste of property or a masterpiece.

Visual and atmospheric variations must be considered when deciding to buy, build, or renovate a beach house. Choices in Southern California range from flat, broad, sandy beaches, to dune beaches, to narrow and rocky beaches. One might choose either a large, expansive cove or a small, uninhabited pocket beach. The height and proximity of mountains and cliffs can also affect the choice, as can the color of the sand, the cliffs, ground cover, and nearby landscaping. In addition, the style of neighboring houses can be incorporated into the design of a new house or can be ignored in favor of something entirely different.

Formally, there are a number of Southern California beach house precedents that offer inspiration and solutions, including the 1920s and 1930s International Style works of European émigrés Richard Neutra and Rudolph Schindler, such as Neutra's Lewin House on Santa Monica's Gold Coast and Schindler's Lovell Beach House at Newport. Architects such as Stiles O. Clements, John Byers, and Roland Coate, Sr., as well as Greene and Greene, who designed many Craftsman-style houses, also built at the beach. They and other revivalists designed houses inspired by images of the Mediterranean, Spain, Greece, Italy, France, and of American bungalows, adobes and pueblos, and New England cottages.

Since the beach inspires adventure, it likewise inspires residents to choose whatever style suits their fancy or their vision of beach house living. The examples that follow include architect- and artist-designed works, a spec house, an owner-renovated bungalow, and a district of landmarked beach cottages. All the beach houses exhibit exceptional craftsmanship and a passion for the elements of earth, air, fire, and water. They also follow a common dictum: If you live in Southern California, the beach is the place to be and to build.

Malibu

Malibu's beach house community developed in the 1920s after Frederick Rindge's widow, Rhoda May, lost the battle to keep the public highway out of the great seaside ranch that Rindge and Matthew Keller developed in the nineteenth century from a Spanish land grant. Rhoda May, nonetheless, triumphed out of the defeat. In 1926, shortly after defending the land—cowhands and rifles at her side—she leased beachfront property to establish Malibu Colony.

Facing Santa Monica Bay with popular public beaches such as Surfrider, Zuma, and Leo Carrillo, the Malibu coast ranges up to eight miles wide. However, it is the unique combination of ocean and mountains that attracts the residents to Malibu, which received its name from the Chumash Indians who inhabited this coast for nearly 4,000 years. Today, this close-knit community is intent on preserving the rural character of its canyons crossed with creeks and roads, which have indigenous names like Trancas, Kanan Dume, Latigo, Tuna, and Topanga, as well as Big Rock and Saddle Peak. From the mountains, Malibu Creek flows down to Malibu Lagoon at Malibu Point where the historic Adamson Spanish-Moorish beach house was built in 1926 by Frederick and Rhoda May Rindge's daughter, Rhoda Agatha, and her husband, Merritt Adamson. Nearby Little Dume Cove, a semi-private pocket beach on Point Dume, named in honor of the Spanish friar Francisco Dumetz, is a much sought-after residential bluff in Malibu with views of Santa Monica and Catalina Island. Paradise Cove, the largest of three individual pocket beaches located on Point Dume, is more public than the other two and features a small pier.

South of Malibu Canyon is a range of small beach house communities, beginning with Carbon Beach, past Las Flores, Big Rock, and Las Tunas beaches, to Topanga State Beach. Carbon Beach, in particular, boasts deep beaches and lots that vary from the standard thirty-by-ninety foot dimension and have provided the opportunity for creative and experimental beach house design.

Following the revival periods of the 1920s, 1930s, and 1940s, traditional New England–, Mediterranean-, and ranch-style houses continued to be built in Malibu Colony. Along old Malibu Road a typical beach house prototype was established in the 1950s, about the time of Craig Ellwood's Elizabeth Hunt House. The layout features double garages at street level that shelter the house from street noise. The house's main living spaces—the living room, dining room, and master bedroom, with children's rooms and kitchens in between—step down to the beach level, taking advantage of the ocean view.

Since the 1960s, modern houses have been built along the Malibu coast. "In particular, Carbon Beach is becoming an architectural beach," says resident Lisette Ackerburg. "There are new houses here by Michael Graves and Gwathmey Siegel, as well as John Lautner, Jerry Lomax, and others, and our house by Richard Meier." In June 1990 Malibu became a city, and already residents are saying they feel an urbane change in attitude and a greater sense of community. "We have a variety of things going on regularly at the civic center. There's been a recent sculpture-in-public-spaces program, and we have swap meets, great restaurants, movie theaters, and

Richard Neutra built the first modern beach house in Santa Monica in 1938; today, the beach is home to many examples of contemporary architecture.

new shops and services," Lisette adds. "You can always find what you need or something to do here without driving into Los Angeles or Beverly Hills."

Unlike the East Coast Hamptons, Malibu Colony is a virtually year-round residential community, so the tradition of seasonal and weekend party-binging has never taken hold. To this day, privacy attracts celebrities to this peaceful retreat, where a line-up of carefully maintained, wind-buffered decks is the typical view from the beach. Most of all, the lengthy twenty-seven-mile coast of Malibu provides its residents broad, sandy beaches for swimming, sunning, and surfing, coves for diving and spearfishing, and deserted coastline for exploring.

Santa Monica

Closer to Los Angeles, Santa Monica—once called Zenith City of Sunset Seas—is distinguished by a five-mile beach sheltered by lofty palisades. This spectacular cliff formation helped to establish Santa Monica as a resort and residential town when Senator John P. Jones of Nevada founded it between 1876 and 1886 with the open ranchlands owned by his partner, Colonel Robert S. Baker. Santa Monica

Pier was built between 1909 and 1921 as an amusement park, to entice visitors to the resort and fulfill a local demand for entertainment, and is still a popular site. The restored Santa Monica Carousel with its festive 1900 Wurlitzer organ is located on the south side, and on the north side lights designed by Santa Monica–based architect Frank Gehry rhythmically dot the pier, making it a recognizable landmark in the evening seascape.

Beach house communities were established below the palisades, along the Pacific Coast Highway, in the early decades of the city's founding. These beach houses continue to be in great demand because they are close to Los Angeles and easily accessible from the Santa Monica Freeway. Until the 1930s, most of the dwellings were small and used as weekend retreats by families from Los Angeles and Pasadena, but over the years most of these wood shacks and bungalows have been replaced by larger homes used year-round.

Some of the most impressive beach houses are found along a short stretch of the Pacific Coast Highway that goes by its original name, Palisades Beach Road. The houses here are often full estates spread over double lots with pools, tennis courts, and guest houses above double garages that face the highway and buffer the main houses from highway noise. This is the Gold Coast where film moguls like Louis B. Mayer, Irving Thalberg, and Daryl Zanuck made their homes in the 1920s and 1930s. Movie stars such as Thalberg's wife, Norma Shearer, and later, Peter Lawford, also lived here. At the northwest end of the Gold Coast, architect Julia Morgan created the New England–style, clapboard Sand and Sea Club for actress Marion Davies.

Self-trained Santa Monica architect John Byers, who had a special interest in Spanish architecture, designed several houses on the Gold Coast around double-height inner courts separating the main house and the guest house. In 1938, architect Richard Neutra built a modern house with a curved, oceanfront bay and pipe-rail detailing for Albert Lewin, a German-émigré producer at MGM. Mae West later bought the house, in which she reportedly let her pet monkeys have free reign.

Venice

Immediately adjacent to Santa Monica is the city of Venice, which has experienced extensive gentrification over the last few decades. Many coveted oceanfront beach houses recently have been renovated or replaced by new ones, although most Venice beach houses are quaint and worn bungalows built between the 1920s and the 1940s, which share space on the boardwalk or the spur streets with 1950s and 1960s apartment buildings.

The roots of Venice are in an early twentieth-century fantasy. In 1904 Abbott Kinney, an heir to a cigarette fortune, came up with the idea of recreating the Italian city for which he named it. He commissioned two architects to design canals, hotels, residences, stores, and offices as Renaissance palaces fronted by pointed-arch loggias on eight miles of beachfront property. Kinney also imported two dozen gondolas and gondoliers to ply the canals. His architectural vision was to provide an inspiring setting for cultural enlightenment by the chautauqua method. Mixing popular education with entertainment, there was to be a steady stream of lectures, concerts, and operas. One of the first operas, *Camille*, was held at the end of Venice Pier and featured Sarah Bernhardt in the starring role.

After the first few years, Kinney experienced financial difficulty with this method so he empha-

sized the beach as a place for amusement. A casino was constructed, and a roller coaster and amusement park were installed. World War I came and went, and still Venice did not thrive. Thus, by 1925 Venice became part of Los Angeles, and by 1930 most of the canals were filled and paved over as streets. The residential character of this former tidal flatlands area changed further when oil wells sprung up in the north, and during the 1960s and 1970s when beachfront property was sold for the boat marina community at Marina del Rey and Marina City. Later, in 1980, another portion of the area was sold for the large complex of Mariner's Village Apartments.

Kinney's grand vision left no great residential palaces. His homes were modest, and some can still be seen where a few of the 1904–1905 canals exist south of Venice Boulevard. However, during the 1960s and 1970s, a community of artists—writers, poets, architects, actors, and a variety of followers of the arts and entertainment industries—established studios in the central area of small offices, warehouses, apartments, and storefronts and along the commercial arcades of old Venice. Over the years, they have added special character and created unique environments in the area—many of which are private building interiors. For a while, architect Frank Gehry had his office on the boardwalk, and although he has since moved to Santa Monica, Venice features his Chiat-Day offices and Rebecca's Restaurant. For over two decades, art galleries and chic restaurants have sprung up among the shops and artist's studios, as in New York's SoHo or TriBeCa.

On weekends, the latest fads in dress, hair, personal locomotion, and portable electronic equipment can be seen along the Venice Beach boardwalk where skaters, skateboarders, bikers, and rollerbladers mingle with the crowds. Weightlifters pump iron at "Muscle Beach" between 18th and 19th Avenues, and along Ocean Front Walk between Rose Avenue and Venice Boulevard there is a steady stream of weekend vendors, comics, jugglers, and performers.

The two most recognized Venice beach houses demonstrate two contrasting versions of the area's artistic edge: Frank Gehry's Norton Residence, based on vernacular imagery and materials, is a free-form artwork in itself; and the classic Doumani Residence, designed by artist Robert Graham, is based on pure abstractions and an elegance of artistic vision.

Hermosa Beach • South Bay

South of Venice and Marina del Rey is Hermosa Beach—part of the South Bay or South Beach, which includes the communities of Manhattan, Hermosa, and Redondo beaches. Hermosa is at the center of the South Bay and, by its 1901 deed, it was established as a family resort. The "cheap amusements of commerce" were forbidden from its two-mile beach playground, held exclusively for its residents and "the sea lovers of Southern California." Charlie Chaplin and his family vacationed in Hermosa, and later Ozzie and Harriet Nelson kept a home here. "Hermosa Beach is like a town that the world passed over," explains resident Dr. Andrea Rich, who lives next door to a small 1904–1907 cottage that was the summer residence of William Jennings Bryan. "There are no big high-rises like in Redondo or Manhattan beaches. This beach reminded me so much of where I grew up on Mission Beach in San Diego, which had a little boardwalk, umbrellas, and a very deep beach. I was overwhelmed by the nostalgia and wanted to be here and not in the isolated colony-type community of Malibu. I thought it would be more fun for my children."

In the 1920s and 1930s, houses went up quickly, but since the beaches of the strand are public, beach-goers always found their way between them, particularly along small spur streets. Walk streets now lead to the boardwalk where many Spanish, Mediterranean, modern and Victorian house styles, both new and renovated, coexist. However, the most typical South Bay beach house is a Craftsman-style cottage.

Local residents like the abundant pedestrian, or walk, streets, which are not accessible to vehicles. "I know my neighbors well and everything is walking distance—restaurants, the drugstore, and little hardware stores," comments Rich. In addition, Hermosa is known for its nationally-televised volleyball tournaments and annual surf festival, which draws participants from all over California. Hermosa residents look forward to the two Fiesta de las Artes, arts-and-crafts shows held on Memorial Day and Labor Day weekends, when massive crowds turn up for volleyball games and craft and food booths.

The community spirit at the beachfront is due in great part to the layout of the landscaped and paved walk streets, which are well maintained and create reference points in the pedestrian landscape. Although many of the amenities—the wide beach, its volleyball nets, the lifeguard stations, and the proximity of the Manhattan and Hermosa Beach piers, as well as the thoughtful separation of bike and pedestrian paths along the boardwalk—were set up at the city's founding, their maintenance and enhancement are clear indications that Hermosa Beach, like Venice, has gone through a great deal of gentrification over the last few decades.

Palos Verdes Peninsula

The large peninsula that forms a major part of the shape of Santa Monica Bay is Palos Verdes Peninsula. By zoning regulations there are no hotels, motels, hospitals, or major industries in either Palos Verdes or Rolling Hills, two of the major cities on the peninsula, which are strictly maintained as all-residential areas.

Perhaps it is this preservation of the original rural character that allows for the sense of history that is still felt in the area. The peninsula was once a rancho of the Sepulveda family and was discovered by Cabrillo—along with all of California—in 1542. Both Point Vincente and Point Fermin, the two major promontories of the peninsula, feature historic lighthouses, and between these two points is Portuguese Bend, a former smugglers' hideaway named for the nineteenth-century whaling company, the Portuguese Company. Trade had been strictly limited under Spanish rule, so smuggling became common practice.

Throughout the nineteenth-century Gold Rush years, houses and adobes were built inland and along Diego Sepulveda's stagecoach route. Only after 1917 did Palos Verdes open up for residential subdivision development, when New York banker Frank A. Vanderlip acquired 16,000 acres constituting almost all of the peninsula. He engaged Olmsted and Olmsted, Howard Shaw, and Myron Hunt to lay out a "Millionaire's Colony"—estates, parks, clubs, elaborate roads, and three model villages. However, after World War I, only a pared-down version was begun in 1922–23. "It's a unique community. The whole layout of the city itself was done by the Olmsted group on their way from California back to the East Coast on the train," says architect Frank Burton Wilson, who worked in the area for

The diverse coastal area of Newport Bay affords a wide range of seaside activities.

many years. Olmsted and Olmsted and Charles H. Cheney laid out a master plan for 3,200 acres on the northwest portion of the peninsula. Of the three model commercial villages planned, Malaga Cove was the only one built.

One of the most beautiful oceanfront homes from this development overlooks Malaga Cove. It is in the grand style of a seaside villa, mixing its predominantly Italianate style with Spanish elements, and is in keeping with the design of Malaga Cove Plaza. Armand Monaco designed this estate in 1928 with Olmsted and Olmsted as landscape architects. Originally the Haggerty House, it has since been converted into the Neighborhood Church.

Spanish and Mediterranean architectural traditions have been maintained on the Peninsula since the period of the Olmsted designs by an independent committee called the Art Jury, established to oversee this mandate. The Art Jury prohibited speculative houses, but finally allowed modern architecture, perhaps as a result of the critical acclaim of Wayfarers' Chapel, Lloyd Wright's modern glass,

wood, and stone masterpiece on Palos Verdes Drive South in Portuguese Bend.

Following the Art Jury's sanction of modern architecture, two leading residential architects emerged during the local building boom years of the 1960s and 1970s—Jack Gray and Frank Wilson. Their modern designs often incorporated the dramatic glass-and-wood formula of Lloyd Wright's chapel design yet continued the traditions of the area by using shingle or tile gable roofs and Palos Verdes stone.

Naples Canal, Long Beach

South of Palos Verdes Peninsula the coastal land mass breaks up around Long Beach. This eleven-mile area has become an important industrial and marine center that includes a fish processing site, location for offshore drilling, and a port for the U.S. Navy. Yet in addition to its reputation as a harbor, Long Beach is also known as an ocean resort community. High-rise residential towers are located along Long Beach Boulevard, which skims the coast. An abandoned bungalow by Pasadena architects Greene and Greene from 1907 looks oddly out of place in the shadow of one of these monstrous residential towers. However, the communities further south have given Long Beach its resort and residential reputation. Solidly designed beach houses from the 1950s and 1960s can be found along Belmont Shore, where four miles of beach extend down the Long Beach peninsula. Adjacent to this area is Naples Canal, the picturesque and tranquil residential canal development that is considered by most to be the best location in Long Beach.

Arthur Parson developed this waterside community between 1903 and 1905, and like Abbott Kinney's Venice, it was planned around a series of canals—which, in fact, are not to be found in its namesake of Naples, Italy. The center of the development is an island in Alamitos Bay, a man-made bay fed by the waters of Long Beach Marina. Unlike Venice, Naples has succeeded as a well-kept pleasure boat community. The canal and beach houses here are both traditional and modern in style. Unlike Kinney, Parson did not dictate a homogeneous style: few houses attempt to be "Neapolitan," although a few are Italianate, and a number of them use nautical imagery in keeping with residents' boats docked outside the front door. The exceptional location has inspired creative designs such as California modernist Ray Kappe's dramatic wood-and-glass Crowell Residence.

Newport: Balboa and Corona del Mar

South of Naples on Newport Bay, a quaint residential beach community, the shoreline is broken up into many areas, including Balboa Island, Lido Isle, the Balboa Peninsula, and further south, Corona del Mar. Now known as the Newport-Balboa Peninsula, the area is a sheltered, marshy lagoon, stretching for five miles from west to east, through which the Santa Ana River flows to the ocean. The upper bay extends inland for three-and-a-half miles and is surrounded by cliffs. Seafarers first came here to trade in cattle hides, as described in *Two Years Before the Mast*, by Richard Henry Dana, who named southern coastal sites like Dana Point and Dana Cove.

Today the lagoon is Newport Harbor—one of the largest small boat harbors in the United States—and descendants of the McFadden brothers, who originally purchased Newport Landing in 1873, rebuilt Newport Pier in 1988. Of the over nine

thousand pleasure craft docked here, many are moored outside residents' year-round beach homes.

The historic small harbor offers a number of delightful nautical features, such as the 1890s Dory Fishing Fleet, still operating at its original Newport Pier location. The Balboa Pavilion is a 1904 building restored as a restaurant and boat terminal for passage to Catalina Island. Shuttling cars and people between Balboa Island and the Peninsula, the 1909 Balboa Island Ferry is a national landmark. And the Cannery Restaurant, located in a 1921 bay-side cannery building, offers a unique industrial marine setting.

Amidst all of these traditional naval designs, Rudolph Schindler's boxy modern Lovell Beach House on the Newport shore must have been especially peculiar in 1926 when it was built. However, it paved the way for other modern design in the area, such as the house Arthur Erickson recently designed on Balboa Peninsula.

"I love the lifestyle of the Newport Beach area," says the resident of the Arthur Erickson house. "We go over to Balboa Island on the ferry with our bikes and we ride on the boardwalk. We also have a little boat that we use. We don't just look at the ocean; we have a beach life at Newport that you can't have at Malibu."

Crystal Cove

Crystal Cove is located on Southeast Coast Highway in Laguna Beach, in an area defined as a marine life refuge, bounded by Corona Beach on the north and Abalone Point on the south. This 12.3-acre wildlife preserve retains the scale and ambience of a 1930s beach resort and features examples of Southern California vernacular architecture. It offers the essence of beach life, the impermanence and freedom that inspired the original 1920s tent communities in Crystal Cove and Emerald Bay.

Crystal Cove is on oceanfront land that was part of the Rancho San Joaquin Spanish land grant of 1837. It was later purchased by James Irvine, the Scotch-Irish settler who made a fortune in merchandising during the Gold Rush. In the 1920s, when the Pacific Coast Highway was extended, tourists sought new horizons. However, Laguna could only be reached by crossing Laguna Canyon—still rural today and, at one point, quite lush and overgrown—until the Irvine family donated three miles of beach land to connect Newport-Balboa with Laguna Beach. In that three-mile span, a trail passed inland, but it reached the ocean only a mile south of Corona del Mar where Los Trancos Canyon drained to the sea. The natural pocket beach here was named Crystal Cove in 1927.

The movie industry soon discovered that this lovely setting and its expanding community of thatched cottages were perfect for recreating a South Seas atmosphere. Since the exotic silent film days of the 1920s and 1930s, Crystal Cove's bungalows and cottages have continued to attract Hollywood's attention. In more recent years, it has been the setting for *Creator,* starring Peter O'Toole, and *Beaches,* starring Bette Midler, who now keeps a beach house in nearby Laguna.

Laguna and South Laguna

With cove beaches, hills, and cliffs that hug almost eight miles of rugged coastline, Laguna Beach and South Laguna are two quaint communities at the heart of the California "Riviera." They bear a striking resemblance to their Mediterranean namesake, both geographically and in the fragrances of their flowers and trees, combined with the savory herbal aromas from numerous small restaurants.

Laguna actually extends beyond these two communities to include the coast just below Corona del Mar in the north and Dana Point in the south. Secluded coves and tide pools are abundant here, as are dramatic high bluffs that attract artists, writers, and photographers. Laguna is renowned for its art festivals, small shops, craft studios, and art galleries. During the winter, there are pageants such as the February Winter Festival of arts and crafts. However, the major event of the year is held each summer, when the city sponsors the Festival of the Arts and the Pageant of the Masters, which features dramatic tableaux with actors posed in living representations of famous paintings.

Romantic and traditional house designs abound in this beautiful area, inspired by the lush growth of Laguna and South Laguna. Although there are a number of single-family beach houses that look more like corporate offices or apartment complexes, these meticulously kept communities are rich with solid beach house designs—either perched above the beach on cliffs or located down near the pocket beaches that extend from Crystal Cove to Emerald Bay and Camel Point.

LECHUZA
POINT
•
MALIBU

LYNN AND STANLEY BYER RESIDENCE, 1983

DESIGNED BY JOHN LAUTNER

INTERIORS DESIGNED BY MICHAEL TAYLOR

This rough concrete version of the California beach house merges with the earth and rises at its central point to mimic the gentle Malibu hills in the background. A timeless earth dwelling, it is anchored at its roof crest by a familial chimney and hearth. Architect John Lautner describes his design of this house for Stanley and Lynn Byer, who decided to make Malibu their permanent residence: "I wanted to suit in every way this rocky point and create a durable, sheltered, livable outlook to the panorama of rocks, coves, beach, and ocean." The design premise may seem simple—to create an earthen-form shelter—but the house reveals itself as increasingly complex, both inside and out. "We achieved our objective by designing the roof as a segment of a tilted cylinder and then cutting the perimeter to give the house an irregular, informal edge, thus producing the timeless, natural look," Lautner explains.

"The site is thrilling. I'd never seen a site like this," Lynn Byer says. "First, we were going to build a little beach house because we had just built a large family home in the city. But when it came time to build, the Coastal Commission wouldn't give us a permit. By the time we were permitted to build, seven years later, our children were grown up, and we began to think

more about protecting the environment. We nearly canceled the project. Stanley said, 'When we look back on our lives, will we be glad that we did or didn't do it?' We decided then that if we were going to build, it would have to be a very special house—a whole environment to fit in with the cove and the setting.

"We brought Michael Taylor out to the site, and he said, 'There's only one person who can build a house with the environment, and that's John Lautner.' John is so conscious of the environment, he first proposed that we live in a bedroom without a ceiling. John truly understands the water and the mountains, and he's able to make you feel like you are living outdoors. Here we feel like our house is part of the rocks and the ocean," Lynn says.

In the main living-dining area, large-span window views and natural materials such as rock, slate, and riverbed boulders harmonize the interior and exterior. "We imported large boulders into the plan to further integrate the whole with the rocky point," says Lautner, who designed the interiors with the late Michael Taylor. During construction, the river boulders—which were first steam-cleaned and sealed to avoid fungal growth—were artfully scattered throughout the house and incorporated into the structure. Floors of concrete and sawn slate were designed to resemble a free-form carpet and polished to glisten like the ocean's surface.

Under the expansive canopy roof, the golden light at early evening casts a mellow spell over the living-dining area, revealing interiors that are not only primitive and elemental but also ethereal and otherworldly. Spiky plants in stone troughs, mill wheels, and ceramic pieces from the Byers' collection of pre-Columbian art add earthy accents to the design. Taylor chose Greek klismos-style dining chairs that reinforce the casual angle of the log-and-rush chairs he designed and placed throughout the house.

The idea of separate defined rooms is non-existent as the free-flowing and asymmetrical character of the interior spaces takes the open-plan principles of Lautner's teacher and former employer, Frank Lloyd Wright, one step further. Lautner's spaces gently, organically unfold into one another both vertically and horizontally.

"I can easily entertain four people here or 150 people. It's like an expandable house," Lynn Byer explains. "During the day, it's casual and wonderful, and at night it's very sexy and glamorous. You could do a black-tie party and be in the right style with it. It's unique in that respect. Also, the living room has cozy nooks with three seating areas, and yet it's all one large, open room."

An enormous river boulder marks the steps from the entrance area down into the living-dining area. A rock-garden courtyard visible through the concave glass wall distinguishes the front entrance.

Above: Slotted skylights bring light into the large living-dining area. Above the conversation areas, Lautner created a mezzanine space, or loft, supported by a textured concrete base displaying the imprint of the wood mold forms of its construction.

Left: From the beach, the colors and forms of the house blend in with the beach and the Santa Monica Mountains. The curved roofline becomes a protective cover over part of the oceanfront terrace where a concrete table surrounded by cylindrical concrete stools is used for outdoor dining. Half-inch-thick glass set into the rocks and terrace walls protects the space from wind and waves yet allows full ocean views. Dotting the terrace, boulders, stone jugs, and spiky plantings echo the shapes and colors of the landscape.

Preceding pages: Beachside exterior of the house.

Following pages: Interior of living room. The sunken conversation area seems literally perched above the ocean.

POINT

DUME

●

MALIBU

ANNETTE SMITH RESIDENCE, 1982
DESIGNED BY WAYNE WILLIAMS

On a high cliff close to the tip of Point Dume, the terrace of French Algerian–born Annette Smith's home captures a view of the uninhabited coast along Little Dume Cove. Beyond the casual umbrella and table on the concrete terrace, a lawn sprawls to the edge of the cliff, and through the trees a path leads down to the cove beach.

Annette's late husband, David Smith, who founded and directed California Institute of Technology's Baxter Gallery, participated in the construction of the house. Architect Wayne Williams and the Smiths wanted to recreate the feeling of a Greek cottage with a white-stuccoed roof that functions as both a sun terrace and a platform for viewing the most beautiful unbuilt areas of Point Dume's coast. The chimneys and domed living room articulate the flat roof, recalling Greek Mediterranean architecture.

"The house is like a tent," Annette Smith explains. "It is solid as a building, but you forget about the structure itself and focus on the outdoors." Glass walls provide the broad garden and ocean views and they give the house its modern appearance. Roof heights and varying building shapes distinguish different rooms of the house and recall a cluster of houses in a Greek village.

In the living room, however, the Greek influence of the sculptural, stucco walls is apparent in the raised fireplace with its built-in ledge and the broad soffit that encircles the domed space. Around the fireplace, a small sofa is draped with an American quilt. Bokara, Persian, and Turkish rugs warm the dark brown concrete floors.

"During the war my French parents moved to Algiers, where I grew up in a very beautiful eighteenth-century Arabian palace. There is a European feeling to the interiors because most of the furniture comes from my family," she explains. Although many of the best pieces stayed with her family in Europe or in her country house outside Paris, Smith combined seventeenth- and eighteenth-century French armoires, Oriental carpets, and an assortment of antique chests and chairs to give the house an old-world feeling. "The house is not formal or pretentious," Smith comments. "You arrive in the garden." She often sets up the outdoor space with tables and chairs for informal luncheon parties.

Annette Smith has frequent houseguests from Europe occupying her guest bedroom. The room is furnished with a seventeenth-century Breton armoire, and a macramé work hangs over the bed. "This is not a decorator's house," says Smith. "Things got placed and they stayed.

The macramé was made by a young friend twenty years ago, and it has been adjusted to many windows over that time. Now it has found a place over the guest room bed."

"Even though David and I both taught at Cal Tech in Pasadena, we made this our main home," she says. The Point Dume landscape was always worth the extra drive from Malibu to Pasadena. Here are barren beaches, cliffs, small canyons, and a house with comfortable living terraces to enjoy it all.

"I'm a nomad by inclination," Smith continues, "so I like living in a tent where the outside is more important than what's inside and I'm surrounded by the view, the blue of the sky and water."

Below: The main terrace is the entrance to the house, and a casual garden walk flanked by lemon trees leads to the outdoor living space.

Following pages: The oceanfront facade reveals the domed living room structure with tinted sliding glass walls that open to the terrace and steps down to the garden.

Top: The two upholstered chairs in the living room are Louis XIV and the small secretary is a rare eighteenth-century Napoleon III coach desk. Placed between the slender floor-to-ceiling windows on the sidewall is a sixteenth-century Spanish monk's chair.

Bottom: A tall eighteenth-century Norman armoire fits into the domed living room space. A doorway next to it provides access to a white-stuccoed stair leading to the roof. Reinforcing the Greek village-like character of the house, the open door leads out to a courtyard through which one must pass to reach other rooms.

Top: A macramé work hangs in the guest bedroom.

Bottom: "This small room is a place for a last-minute guest or for a child.
The sleigh bed was mine when I was a child," Smith says. "It traveled with
my parents back to France after the war, and now it's here with me."

DAVID ANAWALT RESIDENCE, 1988

DESIGNED BY MOORE RUBLE YUDELL

What I wanted was a house that looked like Luis Barragan at Sea Ranch," says David Anawalt. When Anawalt inherited family property on Point Dume, he sought out the firm of Moore Ruble Yudell—which includes Charles Moore, one of Sea Ranch's designers, John Ruble, and Buzz Yudell—to design the house. "Buzz was able to zero in our needs, and he worked out the motifs and where to put the rooms on the hillside site," David adds. "The house simply reinterprets the region's Spanish Colonial traditions," says architect Buzz Yudell.

On the ocean side, tiled roofs step up to the tallest tower, which has its own rooftop terrace protected from the wind by thick parapet walls. Exaggerated arcade forms dominate the terrace, and the angled roof plane soars to the height of the octagonal tower housing the dining room below and the master bedroom above. The master bedroom at the top of the tower is small, and each window offers a view of the cove from the bed. Sunlight pours in from changing directions throughout the day.

On the entrance courtyard side of the house, flagstone paving, a traditional fountain, lush planting, and French doors add to a romantic Spanish atmosphere. Here, an outdoor window located at the entrance door offers the first glimpse of the ocean through a side terrace arcade.

On this west side of the house, the arcade protects the interiors of the house from direct sunlight and offers an ever-changing variety of shade and sunlight throughout the day. This side of the house looks out to a small canyon—filled with native planting of Southern California chaparral, imported eucalyptus, and olive trees—which separates the house from its neighbors.

The house is traditional in its use of pink stucco, white wood trim, and a tile roof, but its abstracted architectural forms—such as the exaggeratedly large arcade forms on the south terrace—betray its modern roots. Echoing the tower shape, the main terrace features a multisided bay with built-in seating for sunning or viewing the cove.

Stepping down the hillside site, a glass-roofed, enclosed solarium is located off the living room. "The high volumes are particularly nice for growing palms," says Anawalt, who cultivates rare tropical palms.

The planar style of the late Mexican modernist Luis Barragan is captured in the entrance courtyard where a loggia is planted with bamboo. Clean-lined, trabeated forms contrast with the traditional Spanish courtyard, where an octagonal fountain trickles water from a sculpted pineapple.

Although the interior space is rich in modern architectural forms, its archways, window seats, terra-cotta tile floors, thick plastered walls, and elegant palms recreate a Spanish past. The double-height living room is like an interior courtyard surrounded by the kitchen, dining room, study, and solarium. "Views throughout the space are intentionally framed by interior arcades and windows," adds Yudell. Only the south side of the room is open, with a wall of windows that overlook the terrace and the splendid view of Little Dume Cove.

"In the morning I can just lift my head from my pillow and check the surf," says Anawalt, who surfs with the Malibu Board Riders. "I couldn't do that anywhere else."

The entrance courtyard flanked by loggia and bamboo.

Above: The side terrace offers ample seating for enjoying the stunning view.

Left: Overlooking the lawn and Little Dume Cove, this modern Spanish Colonial fortress looms large over its cliff-side site.

Following pages: "This is the view from the roof of my bedroom where I can shower out-of-doors," says David Anawalt. The tip of Point Dume is seen beyond Little Dume Cove.

Above: The master bedroom.

Right: Architect Charles Moore calls the double-height, tile-floored, palm-filled living room "an interior courtyard." South-facing windows with window seats overlook the main terrace and bring the cove view indoors. Anawalt's sofas are from Tlaquepaque, Mexico.

CHARLES ARNOLDI AND KATIE ANAWALT RESIDENCE, 1989
DESIGNED BY CHARLES ARNOLDI

Originally a weekend retreat and studio for artist Charles Arnoldi, his wife, Katie Anawalt, and their young son and daughter, this Point Dume beach house has been recently adapted for year-round living. "We built a house [on the beach] in Kauai," Chuck explains, "and after spending two months there last June and July, Katy said 'Why do we live in Venice? We have this great beach house in Malibu. Let's move there.' And we've now been living here full-time for two years."

An artist who is as comfortable working in painting as in sculpture, Charles Arnoldi had no doubts about tackling the medium of architecture. In fact, he used the site for his Point Dume beach house much like an empty three-dimensional canvas. His creation, partly sculptural, includes masses and voids: the main volume is a gray, geometric form with voids of enormous sliding glass doors and occasional, well-placed windows. The painterly part includes the conscious placement of deft strokes—smooth planes of gray concrete terraces that contrast with soft, green lawns, dramatically accented by the bold, blue line of a shimmering lap pool.

The result is a minimalist composition of monumental scale, which is both serene and expansive. The gray, rectangular box is subtly manipulated with metal strips organized on a five-foot module and cut through with fifteen-by-twenty-five-foot sliding glass doors on opposite sides of the house. The muted tones of the structure and the concrete terraces allow the rich natural colors of the landscape to dominate.

Arnoldi designed the house as a studio rather than a traditional house. When both sets of doors are open, the effect is dramatic: the house very nearly becomes more like an airplane hangar than either a home or studio.

During the day, the large sliding doors and other windows let in filtered light to the studio-like living room. A fireplace of gray, raw stucco rises to the twenty-foot height of the space, which is defined by white walls and a black concrete floor.

The oceanfront property had been in Katie's family for some time, and the couple welcomed a home that offered fresh air and sunshine and a place to relax with their children. On the ocean side of the house, concrete chairs and a low table designed by Arnoldi provide an easy-care outdoor place to dine or take in the sun. At one end of the lawn a metal sculpture, also by Arnoldi, is set on an angled concrete base and silhouetted against the peach-colored property wall. Tall grass forms a buffer between the bands of concrete terrace and lawn and the edge of the cliff, and not far out of view a path leads down to the semi-private beach of Little Dume Cove.

A cactus garden and concrete driveway form simple but dramatic sculptural shapes at the front of the house. Arnoldi began his efforts at architecture and furniture design with the design of the restaurant DC-3, but painting and sculpture are his main priorities. Architect Frank Gehry advised Arnoldi on the house's design, and architects David Kellen and Tomas Osinski assisted on the project.

The roof of the house, reached through the galvanized metal sculpture sheltering the stair, serves as a platform for viewing the coast. "The unique thing about living at the beach is that sense of expansiveness—both mentally and physically," says Arnoldi. "You're at the edge of the land, and you have that immense volume next to you." Arnoldi describes sitting in the living room with the fireplace blazing and the sliding doors open to the magnificent ocean view: "It puts you in touch with the elements of nature and the essentials of life."

The small bronze torso is by Robert Graham, and the cast-aluminum fish is by Frank Gehry. Around the low table by Noguchi are a red leather sofa and chair, a steel side table, and a rug—all designed by Arnoldi. The paintings and laminated-and-sandblasted glass compositions of the aluminum doors are also by Arnoldi.

Above: The cactus garden at the front of the house.

Right: Palms, a strip of lawn, and a lap pool form a colorful front courtyard defined on each side by peach-colored property walls.

PARADISE

COVE

•

MALIBU

OLIVIA NEWTON–JOHN AND MATT LATTANZI RESIDENCE, 1993

DESIGNED BY JAMES CHUDA

INTERIORS DESIGNED BY SAUNDRA ABBOTT

When we found this cove setting where sea otters, sandpipers, pelicans, sea gulls, and migrating dolphins and whales can be seen, I knew it was home," explains Australian-born singer Olivia Newton-John about her new Malibu beach house. "I wrote a song about dolphins on one of my albums, and they've been a good-luck sign for me." As the Goodwill Ambassador for the Environment to the United Nations, Newton-John shares a mutual concern about the environment with her husband, Matt Lattanzi, and architect Jim Chuda. Chuda designed the home to represent the latest in environmentally-sound design, both in energy conservation and the use of nontoxic building materials.

"The construction was a monumental task," Lattanzi explains. "All the materials were hard to find because we wanted only nontoxic insulations and paints, recycled and farmed lumber, and selectively logged hardwoods." "The mahogany doors and window casements are from sustainable forestry," architect Jim Chuda adds. "And the oak floors, from private farms in Northern California, are hand-grooved and finished with nontoxic, water-based material."

Chuda, who has known Newton-John and Lattanzi for some time and helped the couple find this particular lot, says, "It is an environ-mental house that integrates nature in a human-istic way. Since it's located in a cove, the five-level structure takes advantage of solar gain and cool ocean breezes, while minimizing slope erosion. Vegetation is added on arbor-covered, natural stone decks to control heat from the summer sun."

"Australians love the beach, and I went to the beach a lot when I was a little girl," says Newton-John. "I like to be near water wherever I live, and my husband comes from Portland where his favorite thing was to go fishing every weekend with his family of ten brothers and sisters."

"Before we built the house, I would sit on the beach site and dream and draw sketches," says Matt Lattanzi. "I wanted the house to be curvilinear and smooth like Mother Nature. I also wanted to have the feeling of a dock, so we terraced the cliff down to the beach level and made a dock at the bulkhead with big, thick ropes. We even shaped the top of the bulkhead so it rolls like the waves."

"Matt built the area down by the beach that looks like a little wharf or pier," Newton-John adds. "He can lower his boat and slide it right into the water." A path, half-hidden by the vegetation, winds down the cliff to the beach and boat dock.

On the inside, a log-beam ceiling and expansive sliding glass terrace doors define the living room space. White slipcovered sofas and an easy chair provide comfortable seating, and Newton-John's white baby grand piano fills one corner. "Olivia and Matt are very sensitive and creative people," says interior designer Saundra Abbott, who also owns Rituals Gallery, "and I feel that the tranquillity of this seaside retreat reflects their spirit. The interiors are filled with carefully chosen antique pieces with a history and life all their own."

"I told Matt and Jim I wanted lots of windows, fireplaces, and balconies where I could put pots and flowers," Newton-John adds about her original request to her husband, who contributed to the design and oversaw the construction with his brother, Chris Lattanzi. "Although it's a southwestern design, it's also Mediterranean in feeling with thick, stark white walls, and big doors. It's a house that feels really strong, like an old fort."

From the beach, curving adobe-like walls and terraces shaded with pine log-and-branch arbors join the house with the cliff. The curved bay holds the kitchen-dining area, and the arbored terrace is located outside the living room.

Above: Casual meals are served in the curved bay of the kitchen that overlooks the ocean. A sculpted southwest-style fireplace with a rough-edge granite surface is used for cooking.

Left: The collection of folk art objects in the living room includes a Daniel Mack armchair crafted in natural maple, a hand-carved New Mexican child's chair, and a mesquite door low table with oxen yoke base. The hand-carved altar candle holder is from Mexico.

Preceding pages: From the guest house, the main house appears perched out on the cliff overlooking the Pacific. A cross-shaped window marks the entrance to the house located under a log-covered arbor.

Peeled pine logs form an arbor structure that frames the Jacuzzi, which is located on the lower oceanfront terrace paved with Chinese green slate. Oaxacan water jugs planted with geraniums dot the terrace, and a small outdoor fireplace is to the left.

MALIBU

COLONY

BEACH

ILENE AND STANLEY GOLD RESIDENCE, 1982

DESIGNED BY RON GOLDMAN AND BOB FIRTH

Designing a spec house can be liberating in many respects. The only restrictions are those of the site and salability; the remaining demands are speculative and creative. Given such an opportunity a few years back, architect Ron Goldman could envision the most appropriate beach house for a setting on Malibu Beach. "I designed the house with Bob Firth, one of my partners in the firm of Goldman/ Firth/Boccato," explains Goldman. "We acted not only as architect and developer, but as builder.

"It surprises me when someone reproduces a house on the beach that can be found in the middle of the city," he adds. "There are issues at the beach that have to be dealt with, such as [taking advantage of] the vistas, the sky, and the mountains, without exposing yourself to the proximity of neighbors. It's a heightened challenge to create openness and privacy at the same time."

Like Cape Cod, Nantucket, Martha's Vineyard, and other East Coast communities, Malibu Colony Beach abounds in traditional, beach-worthy architecture. Therefore, for the typical deep and narrow lot, Goldman and Firth combined angled modernism with the gray clapboard, white-trimmed elements of a New England–style cottage.

"The design is based on the Cape Cod style; it's fairly traditional on the entrance side and more contemporary toward the ocean. It was a balancing act between the traditional and the modern," says Goldman. "Gray is a modern beach color identified with Cape Cod beach cottages. When Joni Mitchell bought the house, she also used a lot of gray on the interiors. Later Ilene and Stanley Gold bought the house, and they've maintained that same gray appearance."

"Beamed ceilings are especially appropriate for a cottage at the beach," Goldman says, and in the monotone gray interior of the living room they add character to the subdued, modern furnishings.

Located just outside of Malibu Colony but sharing the Colony's beach, the house perpetuates that community's established beach terrace format: a raised platform that opens directly to the sand but is protected by a glass or Plexiglas buffer to cut the wind, which creates the feeling of an outdoor living room. Goldman expanded on the tradition by subtly differentiating the dining area, pool and Jacuzzi area, and teak sunbathing platform by floor height.

"On the ocean side, we modernized the conventional New England–style cottage by adding strong roof and window shapes," says Goldman. The glass lanai opens the living-dining areas to the beach, the ocean, and the sky.

While the beach terrace side of the house is open and airy, the entrance to the house is enclosed and tree-shaded—a narrow, trellis-covered English garden. White lilies, azaleas, and camellias, peeling eucalyptus trees, and English garden-style furniture create the idyllic setting of the entrance courtyard. "The recessed entrance door increases openness and light while providing privacy from the neighboring houses," Goldman points out. At night, when the double glass doors to the master bedroom are open, the terrace becomes an outdoor extension of the room, canopied and walled by the darkness. "The absence of walls and ceilings makes the room appear less box-like," says Goldman. Family and guest bedrooms are located on this side of the house, and from this luxuriant, sun-dappled garden, a path leads to the beach terrace.

"Discovery or surprise is a part of beachfront houses," Goldman continues. "Since almost all beach houses back up to a street or an urban setting, the beach is discovered, or unfolds, as the house reveals itself. Each design is, therefore, a juxtaposition or a balance of light and view, of back versus front, of closed versus expansive, or of garden versus ocean."

Transparency and reflection are the themes of the master bath, where an angled skylight in the roof gable brings in an abundance of light and the glass shower stall remains open above to the light and space. The mirrored wall brings the oceanfront view into the bathroom.

Top: Box-like, partially due to the horizontal emphasis of the beamed ceilings, the formal dining room opens up at the far end where an angled, glassed-in space allows both sun and moonlight into the lanai interior.

Bottom: Above the minimalist fireplace in the living room is a work by Frank Stella.

Right: The roof of the double-height master bedroom extends outside to the trellis-roofed terrace overlooking the ocean.

Following pages: The beach terrace is an outdoor living room with spaces differentiated by specific living activities: closest to the house is a dining area. Closest to the beach are the pool and Jacuzzi. At the far end is an intimate place to view the sunset.

The entrance doors are glass, and a triangular window in the gable above recalls
a traditional fanlight.

Bouquet Canyon stone paving is used throughout the ground level of the house, from the street to the pool, to connect the beachfront and garden entrance, as well as the interiors and exteriors of the house.

KRISTI AND DAN STEVENS RESIDENCE, 1968

DESIGNED BY JOHN LAUTNER

This was an extremely difficult assignment, since we requested five bedrooms, four baths, a painting studio, child's playroom, and a swimming pool in addition to the usual living room, dining room, and kitchen," says resident Dan Stevens of the commission he gave to architect John Lautner for his home on a tiny Malibu Colony lot, thirty feet wide by ninety feet deep. "It was a challenge," agrees Lautner, "but the main idea was to provide a joyful, free space with openings to the mountains and the sea, and yet make it private." Seen from the beach, the elegant concrete curves and fan-shaped windows capture the exuberance of Lautner's effort and belie the struggle to accomplish so much with so little space.

The Stevens House is atypical in Malibu Colony. Lacking the traditional gabled roof and boxy shape, it has a greater sense of freedom and elemental simplicity. "To achieve all the spatial requirements we created two segments of concrete catenary curved roofs. These shapes not only go with the waves and mountains but are all in compression structurally to avoid cracking," Lautner explains. "Reversing the curves created openings in the middle of the residence's length, while a typical box-like beach house only opens at two ends."

Through the glazed walls of the concrete curve, a view of the mountains is framed by the structure and its wood window mullions. At the rear of the house, the second catenary curve structure is enclosed for the privacy of bedrooms, a study, painting studio, and kitchen.

The living room is actually small in square footage, but the expansive height and the glass wall overlooking the lap pool and the beach make it appear much larger. A few steps up from the living room, the dining area faces the mountain view through a glass wall at the other end of the open living space. The Stevenses and Lautner finished the living and dining room interior walls in mahogany and cedar and covered the floor in durable ceramic tile. African sculptures acquired by the Stevenses on several trips to Africa are placed throughout the interiors.

The catenary curve structure holding the living-dining area is fully open, allowing light and the drama of the beach into the space of the Stevenses' Malibu Colony house. Instead of a glass or Plexiglas wind buffer and a short flight of steps, typical of most of the homes in the Colony, the Stevenses' terrace is open and free—a simple ladder leads to and from the beach.

From the living-dining space, one set of stairs leads down to the children's playroom and another set leads up to what is now a master suite of rooms. The teak floor and simple furnishings in the beach-facing master bedroom focus attention on the view and the sculptural catenary curve structure.

Four amply-proportioned chairs provide seating in the living room, with a concrete fireplace on the right and ocean views through two abutting glass window-walls. Below the desk, what looks like the glassy surface of an indoor pool is actually a skylight over the children's playroom.

"The house has adapted well to changes in the family over the years," adds Lautner. "For example, several of the upstairs children's rooms have been transformed into a study and a large painting studio for Dan Stevens. And the children have the run of the playroom and bedrooms on the lower level."

"Ever since childhood I wanted to live by the ocean," says Dan Stevens. "You'd be surprised that this stretch of beach is fairly deserted 320 days a year. I dreamed of this kind of peaceful, deserted beach as a child." With the fan shades open, the views from the living room and master bedroom inspire further dreams and offer splendid views of the ocean framed by Lautner's dynamic concrete shapes.

The exterior from the beach, which shows the double shape of the roof.

Left: Steps lead down to the terrace and garden, always full of seasonal blossoms.

Above: For year-round swimming, the forty-foot lap pool is sheltered under a concrete arch patterned with the impressions of the rough wood mold.

Preceding pages: An evening view through the living room out to the beach.

Rancho Malibu LaCosta is a significant Southern California landmark and a fine example of beach house living in the early years of Malibu's development. The Moorish-Spanish Revival residence was built by Rhoda and Merritt Adamson, who were members of two of the founding families of Malibu—the Rindges and the Adamsons. Rhoda was the daughter of Frederick and Rhoda May Rindge, the last owners of Malibu Ranch, the land received in a Spanish land grant. After Frederick's death, Rhoda's mother, Rhoda May, single-handedly fought, but lost, a seventeen-year battle to keep the public highway from reaching Malibu and destroying its private and rural character.

Built on a spectacular beach site on Vaquero Hill overlooking the ocean and Malibu Lagoon, the Adamson House was intended to be used only as a summer home. Picturesque Malibu Lagoon, a small inlet which is home to more than 150 species of birds, is closely identified with the house.

Rhoda and Merritt's grandson Grant Adamson recalls spending holidays there as a child. "That's when I fell in love with the Spanish-Moorish architecture," he says. "I'm in the real estate business in Malibu, and that house is still my favorite. It's kind of romantic and mysterious, and when [I was] growing up, it made a great place to play hide-and-seek."

The elegant peacock fountain in the entrance courtyard is a focal point that can be seen from the entrance hall of the house. A low wall encloses the courtyard and forms a colorful, tiled backdrop for the fountain, which displays two exotic peacocks flanking a freestanding vase. Such romantic images and motifs were typical of the revival period of the 1920s, but they had a special meaning for Rhoda, whose father, Frederick Rindge, treasured the Spanish past and the early years of California and Malibu. In 1898 he wrote *Happy Days In Southern California*, an account of his life on Malibu Ranch, the founding of Malibu, and other legends and lore of the early settlers and local Chumash Indians.

Rhoda's mother founded Malibu Potteries in 1926. For a little more than a decade, the Adamsons used clay from the hills to produce colorful, handmade Mediterranean- and Spanish-style ceramic works and tiles that decorate numerous homes and buildings throughout Southern California.

The Adamson House and landscaped grounds are now owned by the State of California and are open to the public. Visitors can experience the house's rustic California charm and the sophisticated, exotic elements of the Spanish-Moorish design. In the guest bedroom, the Adamsons' coat-of-arms is displayed on the headboards. Here Rhoda's dresses are laid out on the full-skirted, handmade bedspreads, and between the beds, an electrified hanging oil lamp displays the revival-style details Holtzclaw and Clements brought to the house.

The Adamsons kept another home in Serra Retreat until 1936, when they made Rancho Malibu LaCosta their year-round home. Rhoda remained in the house after Merritt's death in 1949, until her own death in 1962. "I always lived within about two miles of my grandmother's house," says Grant Adamson. "Once, as a small child, I walked down to the beach and tried to get in to visit Grandma from the beach but the gates were locked. Later, I told Grandma about it. Her reply was kind of clever and rather typical of her. She said, 'Grant, I'd love to leave that gate open to let the little boys in, but I've got to keep the big boys out.'"

"I got married at the house in 1983 after the state owned the property," recalls Grant Adamson. "Making my entry to the wedding on a jet-black quarter horse, I galloped up the driveway, dismounted onto the low wall of the entrance courtyard, and jumped down. Everyone loved it. My wife and I left the wedding in my grandparents' 1935 black, V-12 Pierce-Arrow."

Today, the house is memorialized and preserved as a California landmark and it is listed in the National Register of Historic Places. The Adamson children, as major Malibu landholders, continue to be active in the city's affairs.

Stiles Clements's masterful Spanish Colonial design for the Adamsons' tiled-roof house features Moorish arched windows, walls of decorative tile, a second-story balcony, and a large entrance courtyard. An outdoor corner fireplace and decorative fountain highlight the courtyard.

Above: The pointed arch of the fireplace is a Moorish motif.
Danish artists Ejnar Hansen and Peter Nielsen painted the decorative pattern on the fireplace hood, which features an image of
Neptune, god of the sea. The patterned tile floor and wood-
beamed ceilings add to the Spanish design.

Right: An antique French dining table is surrounded by leather-
back Spanish Renaissance–style chairs. To create a rich and
glittering setting in the dining room, as well as throughout the
house, designer Holtzclaw used gold-leaf details on the buffet
table, chairs, and mirror frame. The brilliant colors of the tiled
kitchen counter are seen beyond the wood door.

Preceding pages: Broad view of the house.

Top: The peacock fountain features a vivid blue vase against a tiled and arched low wall enclosing the entrance courtyard. The tiled backdrop to the water basin displays two exotic peacocks.

Bottom: Throughout the house, fountains, floors, bathrooms, and kitchen counters are finished in Malibu Tile from the family-owned Malibu Potteries located a half-mile away.

Top: At the tile-paved entrance courtyard, two arched glass doors with foliate-patterned grillwork open to the entrance hall. The undulating loggia ceiling is decorated in motifs devised by Danish artists Hansen and Nielsen.

Bottom: A Moorish star-shaped fountain trimmed in Malibu Tile decorates the grounds. Beyond the fountain is a lifeguard station and the Malibu Pier. The landmark house occupies a stellar location at Surfrider Beach.

CARBON

TO

LAS

TUNAS

BEACHES

•

MALIBU

LISETTE AND NORMAN ACKERBURG RESIDENCE, 1986
DESIGNED BY RICHARD MEIER

"Norman and I saw the exterior of a house in Florida that Richard Meier designed," Lisette Ackerburg explains about the commission for their Carbon Beach beach house. "And we said to each other, 'this is the form, the pristine whiteness we want.' We asked Richard Meier to design the house when he came to Los Angeles to do the J. Paul Getty Center, and now architects from all over the world knock on our door and want to see it."

A disciple of the early-twentieth-century French modernist Le Corbusier, Richard Meier follows the same principals of an industrial-based vision. He can reproduce the same formula of white cubic volumes, curving walls, glass block, square windows, ocean-liner pipe-rail, cylindrical columns, and ramps, but his details betray a constantly changing evolving style.

"The sun, humidity, and salt air can play havoc with a stucco surface," says Norman Ackerburg. "This stucco is an all-cement, steel-troweled type that looks like plaster." Richard Sol, the consulting architect for the project, says, "Norman, who spent forty-four years as a builder, worked through a lot of the construction problems himself."

"My first exposure to living at the beach was through Lynn and Stanley Byer," says Lisette Ackerburg. "Stanley is Norman's cousin, and they had rented at the Colony before building their house with John Lautner and Michael Taylor. When Norman and I married, Norman said he'd also like to live in Malibu. Although we have houses in Palm Beach and Minneapolis, this is Norman's very favorite place. Whenever we plan a trip, he asks me, 'Why are we going anywhere when we have the most beautiful place in the world right on the ocean in Malibu?'"

"It's a privilege to have built a house on the beach," she says. "There is a casualness, a comfort, a privacy. It's like you're in touch with the earth and the heavens, all by yourself—a very private, sensual feeling. People who live in this little compound have the opportunity to focus on their lives."

The Ackerburgs eat lunch outside nearly every day they spend in Malibu. On clear days Norman and Lisette can see all the way to Catalina. "The light and the color of the ocean vary—sometimes it's very blue and other days it's very gray or brown," comments Lisette Ackerburg. "And the beach is different every day. Some days it's piled full of rocks, and other days it's so clean you can clearly see footprints, dog prints or bird prints. The sound of the ocean is very relaxing, very peaceful. When I walk through the doors of my home, I leave the world behind me."

Pieces of the Ackerburgs' contemporary art collection, such as sculpture by Robert Graham, paintings by Dubuffet, Frank Stella, and Ron Davis, and a portrait of Lisette Ackerburg by Larry Rivers, personalize the house. Many of these artists are friends of the Ackerburgs and often share the house with family, friends, and out-of-town guests. The guest house is located at the front of the lot over the garages. "We always have houseguests, but the guest house is so separate that they can come and go as they want without disturbing us."

"Everyone looks forward to coming out to the beach house," Lisette Ackerburg continues. "Last summer, to celebrate Norman's birthday, we had 'Camp Ackerburg' here. Seven grandchildren came for swimming class, tennis lessons, beach walks, and shell hunts. We had music, sing-alongs, and bus trips to Disneyland and other places. Our own camp T-shirts spell out 'Camp Ackerburg' and show a picture of the house."

Just inside the entrance screen wall is an outdoor room—a courtyard defined by the white, undulating wall of the living room and a field of green grass. Meier used a modular unit for the square windows, the paving blocks, and other elements throughout the house. The entrance screen wall and the courtyard shelter the main living areas from street traffic noise.

Above: The fireplace is a bold sculptural entity that separates the living room from the dining room.

Left: In the living room, double rows of clerestory windows and layers of interior walls and exterior sunscreens frame the views and filter natural light into the room. "Bruce Weber, Herb Ritts, and a number of renowned photographers from all over the world come in to photograph, and they all say the light here is spectacular," says Lisette Ackerburg.

Following pages: Facing the oceanfront, a corner wall wraps the inside cube of the house, forming a detached sunscreen that shields it from the sun. The sunscreen frames a bronze sculpture by Robert Graham and defines the outdoor dining area. Meier designed the granite table and the terrace paving to absorb the sun's glare.

A single row of modular clerestory windows punctuates the ceiling line of the living room. The large painting on the left is by Ron Davis, a close friend and internationally-known artist who maintains a painting studio and residence in Malibu.

Meier varied the interior with large and small spaces to create light, shadows, and depth. The double-height living room features a music alcove. Above, a mezzanine library is reached by the pipe-rail stair. The circular light well draws light into the library where a three-dimensional Larry Rivers painting is displayed.

KAREN AND DAVID GRAY RESIDENCE, 1990
DESIGNED BY DAVID GRAY

L as Tunas Beach is very rustic and frankly not as popular as other Malibu beaches. However, I found the rocks and the natural formations in the water to be quite beautiful. And, of course, this location is convenient to my office in Santa Monica," says architect David Gray about the site for his own beach house. However, it turns out Gray's reason for living at the beach came less from the discovery of a rustic location than it did from his wife's passion for beach living. "Karen is the sun-and-sand person," he admits.

"I started out in Malibu when I first moved here from the Midwest," Karen Gray says. "David and I kept moving farther inland to Laurel Canyon, when I finally said, 'I have to go back west. You have to try the beach—I swear you'll like it.' Now I feel like I live in a sculpture of David's design, and every day I wake up and think what a lucky person I am. Here, the light and water constantly change; the tide and sea animals differ daily."

The shoreline is relatively narrow along Las Tunas Beach, so that the saltwater and the sound of the surf are close and, at times, unrelenting. On this sometimes harsh site, the Grays built their beach house. David Gray had designed a number of beach houses up and down the Southern California coast for clients such as Dustin Hoffman and Michael Ovitz. When it came time to design his own beach

house, he knew exactly what he wanted and how to work with the demands of the setting. He used his house as a testing ground to explore both the scenic potential of the site and the tolerance of the building's materials to the natural elements of moisture, sand, and salt air.

"Resistant steel and concrete are the basic structural materials," says Gray, explaining the house's ability to withstand earthquakes, high waves, and wind. "The reinforced concrete pilings are drilled twenty-five to forty feet down into the bedrock, and the house is shielded by a bulkhead that forms the beach terrace." In addition to their strength, exposed concrete, galvanized and stainless steel, treated aluminum, and glass block won't rust or corrode.

The design is organized internally into three horizontal and three vertical sections. Horizontally, the main entrance is located at the mezzanine level, suspended between the kitchen-living-dining areas below and the bedrooms above. Vertically dividing the house at its center, a large steel-and-wire staircase in yellow spans the three stories. The yellow stair terminates at the upper level in a split stair that leads to the master suite on one side and the guest bedroom on the other. There are few interior separations in this open-plan design, and even the walls and doors of the bedroom entrance are made of translucent glass.

"The concrete shell also serves as a solar

collector, absorbing sunlight all day," explains Gray. "At night when we need the warmth, the house radiates the heat." Industrial-style windows open out, venting the house, and at roof level, the glazed gable forms a cross-axis that captures sunlight for the interiors of the passive solar house. On one side of the house, exposed chimney flues and an outside stair are seen against the translucent glass-block windows that allow filtered light into the interiors.

Architectural language and structural detail are well thought-out and unify the exterior and the interior of the Gray house. The rugged strength of the exposed concrete frame is softened by the reflection and transparency of the glass infill walls. Although David Gray's taut metal-and-wire stair and terrace railings may appear more industrial than nautical, his sense of meticulous craftsmanship is worthy of the finest shipbuilding on any coast.

Floor-to-ceiling glass walls reveal the full view of the coast in the guest bedroom, and the window vents open to allow cool breezes. The interior design is intentionally spare—two wicker chairs and a telescope on bare concrete—to allow the focus to remain on the view through the undraped window wall.

Above: The Gray house is eye-catching because of the brilliant color of the Indian red sandstone that fills out the gray concrete frame on the entrance and side facades.

Left: The beach facade of the house, where Karen Gray takes in the sun, features expanses of tinted glass. Small triangular balconies subtly offset the bilateral symmetry and cubic geometry of the design.

Above: Varying light is one theme in the master bedroom, which is partially roofed and partially opened to the gabled skylight, allowing the Grays to sleep under the stars at night. The low-ceilinged area provides relief from the overhead sun during the day, and the glass-block and side windows offer views of changing shadows and light at all hours of the day.

Left: The bare concrete floors and walls of the interior and the yellow, open-tread steel stair with glass-block landings are easily maintained. Most important to the design, the open concrete frame allows all three stories to be viewed simultaneously. The multilevel living areas share the varying light of day and spectacular views.

THE LOUIS B. MAYER HOUSE, CIRCA 1926

DESIGNED BY ADRIAN

INTERIORS DESIGNED BY JOHN COTTRELL

Silhouetted against the palisades and palms of Santa Monica Beach, one tiled-roof, Spanish Mediterranean–style house—home to Louis B. Mayer in the 1920s—helped to establish this area as the Gold Coast. "What is exceptional about it is that MGM's designer Adrian created the house for Mayer," explains the resident who, with her husband and their three children, has owned the home for a number of years. Adrian, the chief costume designer at MGM for many years, designed it like a set, a theatrical interpretation of an opulent Spanish-style house with dark wood beams and moldings.

Today the elaborate house, spacious double lot, tennis courts, swimming pool, and small guest house all remain, but the couple bought the property to raise their family by the beach, rather than to entertain movie stars. "We were living only two houses away so we had already committed ourselves to living on the beach," adds the resident. "My husband and my two sons surf, and we all enjoy water and beach sports. We're outdoor people."

Before they moved in, the residents sought the help of a friend, interior designer John Cottrell. Cottrell gave the house its casual, family character by lightening the interior woods and adding provincial furniture and floral-patterned upholstery and drapery.

The rotunda forms one end of the living room downstairs and the master bedroom upstairs. The large upper deck serves all the upstairs bedrooms, and the loggia located just outside the dining room is used for outdoor dinner parties or casual dining. On the paved terrace to either side of the umbrella-shaded outdoor table are a pair of planters holding rubber trees. The home has now made the transition from Louis B. Mayer's Gold Coast production to a well-used and cared for family home. The family can breakfast or sunbathe on the bedroom terrace with white wood rail and potted geraniums.

The living room, which Mayer used as a small theater, had a full stage under the floorboards that could be made to rise by the push of a button, and a sound and projection booth located at one end. The recessed projection-screen wall is now the perfect location for the residents' prized Oriental screen, and at the bay end, which extends into the beach side of the house, an amply-proportioned conversation grouping joins the baby grand piano.

In the bedroom, the large picture windows and the light, floral-patterned upholstery and drapery add to the traditional seaside-cottage flavor of the room. Louvered shutters can be adjusted to block the morning light coming through the French doors to the upper terrace.

The strength of Adrian's original design is still felt in the structural definition of the living room: the light, oak-beamed ceiling and floral-upholstered valance enhance both the height and the curved bay end of the architectural space. In the dining room, his design of high ceilings and wall moldings gives a formal, classical backdrop to the warm and casual furnishings. Although Cottrell's design has little to do with the Spanish style of the house, he managed to handle the double task of restoring Adrian's original design by removing previous renovations and transforming Mayer's high-living, film-mogul style into the everyday comfort of a family home.

From the upper terrace, each of the bedrooms has a view of the beach and volleyball nets. Below, on the beach side of the house is the Olympic-size pool.

Top: At the curved end of the master bedroom, under a conical, oak-beamed ceiling, a pillowed sofa and large easy chair form an intimate conversation group.

Above: French doors in the dining room open to the loggia, the beach terrace, and the garden.

Right: Behind a high wall and the main gated entrance is a quiet, brick-paved courtyard. Low trees and white flowering plants surround a fountain designed around a classical figure of a cherub.

Preceding pages: Seen from the beach, the rotunda, which contains the living room below and the master bedroom above, is the house's most prominent feature.

The Pacific shore is the front yard for this year-round, urban beach cottage," says architect Steven Ehrlich, explaining his design for a house on Santa Monica Beach, which has Palisades Beach Park as its backdrop to the east. The house enjoys views of the historic Santa Monica Pier to the south and the mountains above Malibu to the north. "It takes full advantage of the beachside vistas," continues Ehrlich, "by juxtaposing expanses of wall with large areas of glass." The result is fairly industrial: the steel-frame exterior is made of steel-troweled stucco with aluminum reglets below and white stucco with glass tiles above; the gabled standing-seam roof is a matte gray, galvanized metal; and garage doors open the house's ocean side. The lot is a narrow, eighteen-foot-wide strip of land between Pacific Coast Highway and the beachfront promenade, wide enough for the two-car garage. The forty-five-foot height allowed for three stories.

The height of the project is accentuated by what Ehrlich describes as the "beach cottage"—a single room located on the third floor, reminiscent of California's vernacular, one-room vacation hideaways. The upper "cottage," which encloses the master bedroom, features a glass-filled gable with a front porch–like terrace on the beach side. The glazed garage door dominates the middle-level beach facade. When the shade is down, it appears opaque and similar in tone to the sidewall of translucent glass tile. Ground level walls are fully enclosed and designed as a base for the rooms above. Since the location is a popular public beach, the blank lower walls add needed privacy.

"The floor plans are organized by a three-part sequence of areas and volumes," adds Ehrlich. "These volumes are expressed on the exterior by the vertical voids in the side wall, which introduce light and definition of space to the interior."

Inside, textured surfaces and metal strips on the living room fireplace repeat the theme of the exterior design. The chimney flue is covered by a triangulated box made of translucent glass tile, adjacent to the shoji screen effect of the glazed sidewall. In the morning this translucent sidewall floods the space with light.

The living-dining loft space is the heart of the house. A mezzanine and an open stairway define two sides of the eighteen-foot-high living room. "At the top of the stairs from the living room, a hanging landing leads to a loft," explains Ehrlich. "It's like a suspended bridge in a cubic, glass-walled space, because the vertical circulation is silhouetted against translucent panels. The translucent materials let light in but seclude the Israels from the urban environment."

The resident, writer Neal Israel, likes living in a beach house for two reasons: the air quality and the opportunity to run on the sand. But finding this particular house seemed a perfect fit for his life, like several other serendipitous events that have occurred to him. "Neal and I met through NBC's 'Man of the People,'" says his wife, Romy, of the TV show that brought them together—a series that Neal wrote, in which she acted. "And when the show finished, the large pool hall painting from the bar set happened to fit our living room wall perfectly."

"Neal fell in love with the house," continues the actress. "He was pretty emotional about it because he feels if you live in California, you should live on the coast. It's just a better life."

The glass garage door opening extends to the second-story living room to allow a view of the beach. "The broad sixteen-foot-high sectional glass door can roll up completely to the ceiling, erasing the boundary between living room and outdoors," Ehrlich adds.

Above: The street side of the house is enclosed, with only a simple slit opening at its upper level and translucent glass at the middle level.

Left: Since the location is a popular public beach, the blank lower walls add privacy. The middle level is dominated by a glazed garage door, and the top floor is treated as an added-on beach cottage.

Top: The contrast of light and shadow plays a changing role in the living room loft space where a gangster painting from the Israel's art collection adds a dramatic touch.

Bottom: A pipe-railed catwalk attached to the translucent sidewall passes through the double-height space. The small maple desk and chair were designed by Marlo Ehrlich.

Right: The glass-topped table and chairs, also designed by Ehrlich, are constructed from the same rich maple used for the floors and cabinetry.

ANNETTE SMITH RESIDENCE, 1982
DESIGNED BY WAYNE WILLIAMS

On a high cliff close to the tip of Point Dume, the terrace of French Algerian–born Annette Smith's home captures a view of the uninhabited coast along Little Dume Cove. Beyond the casual umbrella and table on the concrete terrace, a lawn sprawls to the edge of the cliff, and through the trees a path leads down to the cove beach.

Annette's late husband, David Smith, who founded and directed California Institute of Technology's Baxter Gallery, participated in the construction of the house. Architect Wayne Williams and the Smiths wanted to recreate the feeling of a Greek cottage with a white-stuccoed roof that functions as both a sun terrace and a platform for viewing the most beautiful unbuilt areas of Point Dume's coast. The chimneys and domed living room articulate the flat roof, recalling Greek Mediterranean architecture.

"The house is like a tent," Annette Smith explains. "It is solid as a building, but you forget about the structure itself and focus on the outdoors." Glass walls provide the broad garden and ocean views and they give the house its modern appearance. Roof heights and varying building shapes distinguish different rooms of the house and recall a cluster of houses in a Greek village.

In the living room, however, the Greek influence of the sculptural, stucco walls is apparent in the raised fireplace with its built-in ledge and the broad soffit that encircles the domed space. Around the fireplace, a small sofa is draped with an American quilt. Bokara, Persian, and Turkish rugs warm the dark brown concrete floors.

"During the war my French parents moved to Algiers, where I grew up in a very beautiful eighteenth-century Arabian palace. There is a European feeling to the interiors because most of the furniture comes from my family," she explains. Although many of the best pieces stayed with her family in Europe or in her country house outside Paris, Smith combined seventeenth- and eighteenth-century French armoires, Oriental carpets, and an assortment of antique chests and chairs to give the house an old-world feeling. "The house is not formal or pretentious," Smith comments. "You arrive in the garden." She often sets up the outdoor space with tables and chairs for informal luncheon parties.

Annette Smith has frequent houseguests from Europe occupying her guest bedroom. The room is furnished with a seventeenth-century Breton armoire, and a macramé work hangs over the bed. "This is not a decorator's house," says Smith. "Things got placed and they stayed.

POINT

DUME

•

MALIBU

VENICE
BEACH

Architect Frank Gehry once lived and worked in Venice, and he still spends a lot time there. In the forefront of Venice's gentrification movement, Gehry renovated a space for his office on a boardwalk site only ten minutes north of the site of the house he later designed for friends Bill and Lyn Norton. It was Gehry's intention to design the house to fit the context of the eclectic neighborhood. He chose diverse exterior materials including concrete block, ceramic tile, stucco, and wood logs. The result reflects the variety of textures and colors that form this complex urban context. "The house says so much about Venice," says Lyn Norton. "Frank understands the constantly changing community, and the house reflects that. For instance, one side looks as if the building was sheared off and demolished, or just in construction."

Daily living is quite an experience in Venice, where one's neighbors can vary from a record executive to a couple on food stamps or an aspiring actress who waits tables at Rebecca's or 72 Market Street. "People say, 'How can you bring up a child in Venice? It's so dangerous and so dirty,'" says Lyn Norton. "But our twelve-year-old son sees many sides of life and a racial mix. And our house is south of all the worst of the craziness."

"We used to live on the Grand Canal," she adds. "But it was Bill's dream to live on the beach. He knew Laddie Dill and other Venice artists from their surfer days, and he met Frank Gehry through them." Bill Norton explains, "I always wanted to live on this particular beach. I knew Frank and had previously backed a project with Chuck Arnoldi and Laddie Dill that Frank designed—the Venice triplex where Dennis Hopper now lives."

Gehry, who studied art in college and counts many artists as his closest friends and associates, always approaches his work as an artist. "I designed a blue-tiled box structure that forms the ground-floor base for the simple stacking of interior spaces. The freestanding study, which echoes the form of the nearby lifeguard stations, is the powerful compositional element," says Gehry.

"At one point in the design, the front tower was a free-hanging loft inside the house," says Lyn Norton. "Frank wanted to include a little jewel or gem, as he described it, that we would all look out on," Bill Norton adds. Gehry wanted to balance the elevation at the back of the house, but he never completely made up his mind as to what the form would be until the house was in construction. After a few designs, he came up with a simple box that echoes the lifeguard towers on the beach. "It was an ironic touch," Bill Norton continues. "I'd told Frank how I loved the beach, sitting in my lifeguard tower reading when I worked as a lifeguard during college, and that solitary work had made it easy for me to become a writer."

"The wide second-level deck acts as a visual buffer between the boardwalk and the living-kitchen-dining areas, and it is contiguous with these areas when the glass doors are open," says Gehry. Living areas and additional bedrooms on the second and third levels are raised from the street and set back from the beach-front walk to increase privacy and allow space for the terraces fronting the house.

"However, our bedroom is near the front of the house," says Bill Norton, "and at night we hear the waves. Sand is very resonant, and you can feel the vibrations of the waves and the surf. It's kind of awe-inspiring to feel the natural power of the ocean."

To increase privacy, the oceanfront deck steps down to the French doors at one end of the long and narrow living-dining room. Gehry's interiors are low-key and structural, without traditional architectural ornament: the stairs continue into the wood-floored interior, and the tiled fireplace is tucked in the corner. The Nortons acquired the bench on a trip to Africa's Ivory Coast, and the painting above it is by Lyn Norton.

"The house is a three-story structure built on a typically narrow beachfront lot, bounded by the heavily-trafficked boardwalk on the beach side," says Gehry. "So the Nortons requested access to the ocean views without sacrificing seclusion from passers-by and neighbors to the north and south."

Above: "We wanted the house to be fairly private, and Frank designed a way to keep the living areas at the back of the house. He lowered the kitchen so that the view is limited to the horizon and the front area of the beach," Bill Norton explains. "We are probably the only place on the beach that hasn't enclosed every square foot," Lyn Norton adds. "And when we want, we can go to the tower and look out over the crowds. It makes it actually very pleasant to be on the boardwalk."

Left: Serving as pedestals for ceramic pots, truncated columns march upward alongside the tile-and-pipe-rail stair linking the third floor bedrooms to the uppermost roof deck.

Above: A studio for Lyn—a painter, musician, and script supervisor—is located at the front of the house and is faced by a ceremonial gateway, a trabeated structure of unpeeled logs.

Left: In the living-dining area the unfinished appearance of the exposed studs resembles an attached greenhouse and "makes a positive connection with the neighborhood," Gehry says. "And the deep skylight offers visual access to the third-floor bedrooms and opens up the long, narrow living area."

Above: Bill Norton, a former Venice Beach lifeguard, is a screenwriter, and his lifeguard station–style writer's garret has become a noted Venice landmark. A stair leads from the western edge of the second-story deck to the tower. The oceanfront and side windows are shaded by raised wood panels, but the glazed entrance wall is fully open, exposing the wood structural elements.

Left: "I mainly direct now, but I still write in the tower," Bill Norton continues, "and often when I get up in the morning, out of habit, I'll go to the tower to look out at the ocean and check the size of the waves, the level of the tide, and the strength of the wind."

CAROL AND ROY DOUMANI RESIDENCE, 1982
DESIGNED BY ROBERT GRAHAM

Having a sculptor design a house can be both a risk and a controversial statement—risky, because an artist lacks training in structural design and experience in building, and controversial, because some critics and architects (perhaps out of jealousy) find it almost unethical for an artist to experiment with the three-dimensional and practical aesthetic of architecture.

The home sculptor Robert Graham created for Roy and Carol Doumani was successfully completed in 1982, and since then has received much acclaim, but Graham did not work alone. Architects and engineers translated his designs and the sculpture-like wax model he built into blueprints, and he and the Doumanis invited other artists to work within the framework he had created to design site-specific artworks as permanent parts of the structure—doors, windows, cabinets, railings, and so on. As such, Doumani House is an exceptional monument to architectural integrity and classic repose in a neighborhood not particularly known for either.

"Roy and I met Bob Graham shortly after we had begun planning to build a house in Venice," explains Carol Doumani, a writer. "Roy had bought the property on Yawl Street, a corner lot fronting the beach, because of its proximity to the Marina Channel, accessway to the ocean for the seven thousand boats harbored in Marina del Rey. When we asked Bob to create a piece of sculpture for the house we were planning, he proposed designing the whole house instead. His concept was to incorporate his own art as well as the work of other artists as structural and permanent parts of the building, much the way artists worked in the Renaissance. We were thrilled by the opportunity to have him design our house, and we were impressed by his humanist idea of having the art in the house be more than just beautiful to look at, to have it be an integral part of our lives.

"As we worked together on the plans, we strove for purity of aesthetic and design. Bob discouraged us from using an interior decorator," Carol Doumani continues. "What we all wanted was to have the house, its art and its decor, reflect who we are and how we live. For instance, Terry Schoonhoven was painting the mural around the skylight the day my parents brought in my harp, which they had kept for us during the construction of the house. Terry's response to this was to alter the colors in his work to lend a Renaissance feel to the mural, so that it would complement the harp music. And in the living room, there is a low glass table that Dewain Valentine designed. Over the years, when he and his wife, Jina, have come to dinner, as we've sat around the table we've realized it could be more functional, and Dewain has reworked his original design several times to make it perfect for us. Overall it has been an enriching experience for us to watch and learn from the artists who have worked in our house. Through the process many of them have become close friends."

The house is built of stark white plaster and dark glass in the shape of a rectangular block. The entrance, off a walk street, uses a standard baroque formula of a doorway in a U-shaped recess, reached by a flight of stairs and flanked by side wings. Windows designed in a stepped-shape are gridded so that they resemble those of the traditional artist's garret, and their dark tint takes black bites out of the interior corners of each wing. The double entrance door is also designed in a grid pattern, this time of stained-glass panels designed by painter David Novros. Surrounding the recessed base of the house is a lively stainless steel grillwork by Billy Al Bengston. The handrails, door baseboards, and door moldings throughout the house are brass, which has been patinated to balance the bronze sculptures throughout the house.

"Bob's design eliminated the beach balcony common to houses in this area, because he felt it would disrupt the architectural harmony and set the house too far from the sand," Carol Doumani explains. "So Roy came up with the idea of creating an interior balcony, and putting counterbalance weight on the big window so the lower third of the glass could easily be raised. We love to sit in the window and watch the world go by."

The placement of sunken boulders in Michael Heizer's *Displaced Replaced Mass*—much like a Zen garden or, more formidably, floor tombs in a medieval church—intuitively reminds visitors they are entering hallowed ground resonating with the power of many artists' labors. The house has been bequeathed to UCLA, and the Doumanis have established an endowment for its continued maintenance when it becomes the property of the university.

In the kitchen, Tony Berlant created a door from his trademark materials, found pieces of tin and tiny nails, and Bengston designed the wood-inlaid cabinets. All the art in Doumani House is designed to be used. "Every time I'm working in the kitchen and open one of Billy's cabinets, I feel enriched by his art," says Carol Doumani.

Above: Carol Doumani often reads and relaxes in the enormous beachside window of the living room.

Right: David Novros's stained-glass entrance is an abstraction of the dramatically colorful December sunsets at Venice Beach. (On the facing wall, Novros painted a fresco that reflects the same abstract imagery.)

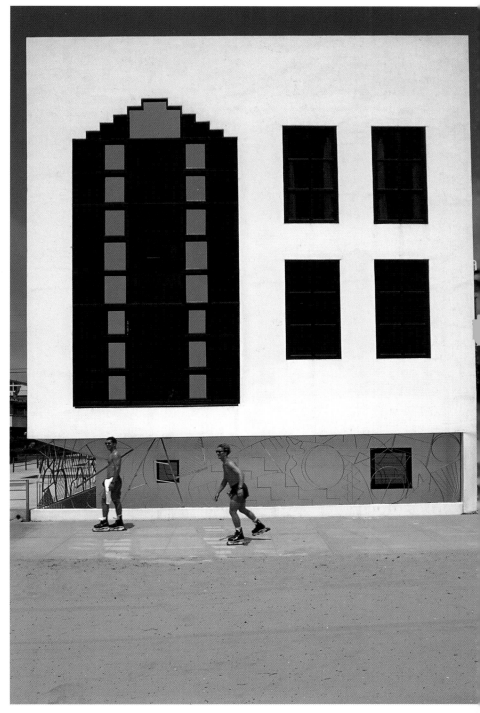

Above: On the beachside, skaters traverse a path called Ocean Front Walk. On this facade, Graham's simple asymmetrical composition is a calm balance of black and white, a pattern of four rectangular windows and a twenty-five-foot-high window, stepped at its crown.

Left: From the street side, the white-stuccoed structure is a U-shaped design with a central recessed entrance flanked by side wings with stepped windows. Billy Al Bengston designed the stainless steel grillwork at the recessed base of the house.

Top: On the third floor, an engraved glass rail by Bengston repeats some of the forms of his exterior grillwork. The interior balcony provides uninterrupted open space for the living room window to span the second and third stories.

Bottom: The music room is on two levels. Ed Moses designed the large window in the intimate alcove used for listening to performances on the harp and piano.

Right: The waterfall skylight designed by Eric Orr creates an organic and rhythmic pattern of reflections on the wall of the double-height music room, where a number of bronze figures by Robert Graham are lined up on tall pedestals against the rear wall.

HERMOSA

BEACH

•

SOUTH

BAY

PAUL AND JANICE SHANK RESIDENCE, CIRCA 1926

RENOVATION BY PAUL AND JANICE SHANK

Among a hodgepodge of different styles along the Hermosa Beach strand, it is rare to find an older house with true design integrity. However, Dr. Paul and Janice Shank's house, crafted slowly over thirteen years by its owner, is the kind of architectural gem that brings new respect to the phrase vernacular architecture. The house was originally built in the 1920s when bungalows had just become fashionable. "The house was originally a chalet-style bungalow," says Dr. Shank. "When we bought it in 1980, it was a basic beach house in poor repair. Over the years we've remodeled it and three years ago we added the third story."

Located on a corner site, the cedar-shingled house enjoys the added space of a pedestrian

Overall exterior view.

street facing the entrance door. "Six years ago two carpenter friends from England helped put the large lintel over the entrance," adds Paul Shank. "We designed it as a simple Oriental touch that was fitting to the Craftsman style." The house is placed on one side of a narrow thirty-by-ninety-foot oceanfront lot, allowing space for a brick-paved courtyard. The deep color of the reddish-brown brick wall matches the rich color of the cedar shingles. "The cedar shingles had been painted over, and shortly after we bought the house we sandblasted them back to their natural state. Also, we replaced the plain windows with windows designed to the scale of the house. We planned the clear lower section and upper lights to a dimension appropriate to the scale of the house."

At the oceanfront, melaleuca trees have overgrown the garden wall. "The brick wall was original but we added the brick paving and the river-rock details," says Paul Shank about the L-shaped courtyard, which exudes the feeling of an English garden—one inspiration for the Craftsman aesthetic. "Janice designed the gardens and courtyard area," Dr. Shank says proudly of his British wife. "However, Janice hates the beach. I love it," he admits. "She likes more privacy, and I'm the opposite. I like the communal spirit of the beach. But we can go upstairs to the family room and get away. Double-paned glass doors keep the noise out. Our children love it. They've grown up here and have no other home to compare it with, but every time they've taken a trip, they come back and say they're glad we live here.

"There is still so much more to do," he adds. "Our philosophy was to live in and evolve with the house. To use the analogy of doing a painting, you have to come back to it and then decide what is needed."

Redwood paneling in the living room is detailed with glass-fronted bookshelves and wood-button pegs. The leather-cushioned rocker and chair were designed by L. and J.G. Stickley.

ANDREA RICH RESIDENCE, CIRCA 1926
RENOVATION BY FRANK ISRAEL, 1992

To associate one of California's leading modern architects with a shingled, vernacular design in South Beach is quite a leap. But Dr. Andrea Rich's Hermosa Beach home was, in fact, renovated by architect Frank Israel. "We remodeled and added onto an existing house," says Israel, who took on the project as a favor for a friend. "It's clad in shingles on the ocean side facade to acknowledge the harshness of the beach. The other facades are in stucco colored to reflect the palette of sand, sea, and sky."

"Frank and I both are committed to modern, clean-line design, and he designed my very modern condo in town," Dr. Rich explains. "But for the beach, I wanted to combine that style with the sense of beach, of home, of weekends, and warmth and relaxation. The house is a row house stuck in between others, but Frank found ways—as only Frank can do—to create skylights and stairwells with light shafts to let in the sun.

"I got this house about eighteen years ago to spend weekends with my young children," she continues. "It had no style to it, and Frank, who is quite passionate about good design, kept saying, 'Andrea, you owe it to the public to do something with this house. Twenty thousand people a day pass by here. It's your aesthetic duty.' Since he remodeled it, it has personality and character."

The house is right on the boardwalk, part of the active life of the community. "Either you're a beach person or you're not," adds Andrea Rich. "I grew up in San Diego, and the idea of being at the beach—that little strip where the water meets the land—was very important to me. I felt very claustrophobic being too far inland, and it had been a life dream to get a place at the beach."

"The third level, which was added, is actually an outdoor room, though it appears to be enclosed space on the beachside facade. This outdoor terrace commands views of the beach and Palos Verdes Peninsula beyond," Israel explains. "It's the major living space and amenity in the house, which includes an outdoor dining area, a Jacuzzi, and a trellis roof that will soon be overgrown with bougainvillea."

On the spacious, open-roof terrace side, windows open upward in a typical beach-shack manner, and the shingled wall and windows buffer the dining area from the wind. "The roof terrace is just paradise," Rich says. "It's like being both inside and outside. There's no roof, but you have protection from the wind. At the same time you get the feeling of being on an ocean-liner. My children and I have traveled the world on ships, and because the terrace room is so high, when you look out you get that same sense and actually feel closer to the ocean than when you see it from the ground floor."

Inglenook-like built-in seats are located on either side of the front terrace windows. Wide enough for one, each provides an intimate, solitary place to watch the ocean, the boardwalk, and beach-goers. It also frames views of the nearby lifeguard station and Hermosa and Manhattan piers.

"From the terrace, you get one perception of the oceanfront environment," says Andrea Rich. "There, I'm removed from the world and can see distances—Manhattan and Hermosa piers, Point Dume, Palos Verdes, and Catalina Island. But from the first-floor living room and terrace I see a parade of people, beach umbrellas, and sailboats. Depending on my mood, I can participate in either world."

A glass-topped wicker dining table and streamlined wicker chairs update the Craftsman-style design in the third-story, outdoor room.

Top: "The fireplace in the master bedroom was rebuilt in raw natural plaster to capture the freestyle mood of the southwest or the Greek Isles," says Israel. An exposed wood-beamed ceiling and simple wood valance suit the beach cottage tradition.

Bottom: "My bedroom had been on the alley side, so a major objective of the renovation was to give me a space right on the ocean and to make it airy," explains Dr. Rich.

Israel's shingled facade subtly resembles an updated Craftsman-style residence. With the addition of the upper terrace and layered front wall, it abstracts the elements of that ad hoc, vernacular style. The shingles, balconies, window shapes, and trellis respond to the neighborhood context.

RANCHO
PALOS
VERDES
•
PALOS
VERDES
PENINSULA

return each year to visit Crete where I was born and raised," says Katina Torino. "I've always lived near the water, and now Rancho Palos Verdes is my home." The views from her residence show the rich yellow color of the land, high cliffs pitched over the sea, and lush and colorful natural landscaping.

Katina Torino's property is considered one of the best on the Palos Verdes Peninsula. The house was designed by the firm of Frank Burton Wilson, one of the leading architects working in Palos Verdes during its building boom of the 1960s and 1970s. "We completed between fifty and one hundred houses in the area. When the job came up, I was so overloaded that I put Richard Huddleson in charge," Frank Wilson explains. "He had been one of my talented students at USC, and I knew what he could do. Huddleson came on the scene while we were having a difficult time getting the project through the Art Jury—one of the most restrictive independent building review boards around."

"When I took on the project they already had a design in the works," says Richard Huddleson. "I felt we had to go back to the basics of laying it out, and my whole point was to make it a mixture of glass, stone and tile. I wanted to get something that looked indigenous to the property. On the entrance side, it looks like the house is growing out of the site, with lots of stone and battered walls. On the ocean side, it has as much glass as possible. We also stepped up the living room to try to take advantage of the view. The platform is a bit unconventional, but it made a tremendous difference in the view from the living room and main living areas. We tried to keep the plan and the structure as simple as possible, and Katina's being a structural engineer was very helpful."

Like Lloyd Wright's nearby Wayfarer's Chapel, the house resembles an open pavilion infilled with glass and glass clerestories. The patterned wood-and-glass doors, recently added, were designed by Mrs. Torino. Glass walls bring the natural ocean-side setting into the living room where Mrs. Torino contrasts formal furnishings with the informal materials and the casual pavilion style of the house.

The side terrace contrasts with the relaxed California style of the stone-and-glass pavilion. Paved in a random pattern of Palos Verdes stone, the terrace features a French parterre filled with roses. A flight of stairs leads up to the breakfast terrace.

"I laid some of the stone for the breakfast terrace myself," recalls Frank Wilson. "The stonemasons didn't understand the pattern that we wanted, so I went up on the hill and showed them. That particular pattern was unusual in Palos Verdes, where they ordinarily set the stone in a random, non-coursing manner." "At that time the main Palos Verdes quarry had been quarried out," adds Huddleson, "but Palos Verdes stone is actually available from other places, and the Torinos found it at a different location."

Angled pine trees bent by the wind and colorful ground cover can be seen growing over the spectacular bluff site. From the house's multiple terraces, Katina Torino enjoys one of the most unspoiled, natural sites on the Southern California coast.

Below: "My sister is an architect, and she recently redesigned the side terrace," Katina Torino says of the formal terrace.

Following pages: The main upper terrace provides a viewing podium for the living-dining wing of the house. The glass-walled master bedroom is located above, with the balcony to the right. Below is the kitchen with its own terrace.

Top: Pots of pink geraniums embellish a low Palos Verdes stone retaining wall that surrounds the main terrace to the living-dining wing of the house. The main terrace is paved with honey-colored terra-cotta tiles.

Bottom: Adding to the spacious quality of the dining room's pavilion-like interior, the dining table is glass-topped with a wrought-iron base. Cane-back chairs and a French tapestry contribute additional texture to the setting.

Preceding pages: The main upper terrace commands a spectacular view of the Pacific.

Top: Traditional and period pieces are displayed against the rugged stone walls, and antique carpets adorn the oak-plank floors.

Bottom: The kitchen terrace is furnished with a round glass table. A pine tree bends over the terrace, which is protected by a Plexiglas wind buffer and paved in patterned Palos Verdes stone.

RONALD AND SUSAN CROWELL RESIDENCE, 1976

DESIGNED BY RAY KAPPE

For the California yachtsman, Naples is an ideal community. One can dock a boat outside the front door and have easy access by canal to Alamitos Bay and Santa Monica Bay. Another major advantage, the privacy of a pedestrian community, is one reason Dr. Ronald and Susan Crowell love living in Naples. "We like the privacy, the tranquillity of the canals," says Susan Crowell. "There are no streets; it's just peaceful and quiet. We're both busy professionals so we appreciate that. It's also a wonderful walking community—very friendly but private."

The Crowells' residence is by the architect Ray Kappe, whose architecture is modern yet timeless. The house is made of traditional natural materials—redwood and brick—and the modern glass elements are tinted a warm bronze to harmonize with the redwood. Here, Kappe worked with the theme of dramatic verticality to capture unobstructed views to the bay and ocean. "The corner-supporting redwood walls leave consistent ten-foot openings, which are filled by fixed glass, sliding doors, decks, stairs, or service elements," he explains.

"We saw the house first from the canal bridge," Dr. Crowell recalls. "It was so special and dramatic—one of the most fabulous pieces of architecture. The kind you'd never dream you'd ever live in." The Crowells bought the house in 1986, but it was designed a decade earlier for Dr. Sidney Penn. Much of the credit for its design belongs to Dr. Penn, who commissioned the house and worked out his ideas with Kappe. When he had to sell the house, Dr. Penn was very concerned that the new owners would care about it as much as he did. The Crowells convinced him they did indeed care.

"Built on a thirty-by-one-hundred-foot Naples Canal site, this residence covers the entire buildable area and reaches the allowable height," architect Ray Kappe explains. "Every room has a deck, and all roofs are usable as additional deck space."

The successful pleasure boat canal community of Naples, located in Long Beach, suites the Crowells well. Along the canals, imported gondolas with singing gondoliers maintain a profitable tourist trade. These gondolas can be rented for tours or romantic evening dinners. "Couples also get married on them," says resident Dr. Ronald Crowell. "And they often stop and look at our house. The light just dances off its bronze glass in the evening sunset."

"What was so serendipitous was that we began collecting Northwest Coast and Inuit art at about the same time we bought the house," Ronald Crowell says. American Northwest Coast art is displayed in the first-floor living room, and the third-story study features primitive pieces from a variety of different cultures.

"The lighting in the house is the best for viewing the types of art collections we have," says Susan Crowell. The lively collections in these warm, cedar interiors vie for attention with canal and ocean views seen through ten-foot wide sliding glass deck doors. "Northwest Coast artists carve in cedar and live in cedar houses," adds Dr. Crowell. "What could have been better than to display the works in the house's rough cedar interiors. It's like living in a cedar longhouse tipped upright."

In the living room, located off the teak entrance deck, a seating arrangement of white sofa, chaise, and ottoman faces a unique melon-colored Navajo rug and a triangular low table holding a Northwest Coast bronze frog by Robert Davidson, "one of the premier sculptors and carvers of Northwest Coast art," says Mrs. Crowell. Masks on the fireplace ledge are Northwest Coast and the contemporary glasswork is by Jonathan Kuhn.

Above: The third-story study offers canal views through ten-foot glass deck openings. An African mask is displayed on the corner fire-screen ledge, and a wood sculpture from New Guinea is on the floor before it. Beside the chaise longue—draped with Indonesian fabric—are African baskets. The cane chairs surround an onyx-surfaced round table holding an African elephant.

Left: The angled, interlocking cubic volumes maximize the view from every room. A wood deck provides an entrance platform to the house where a tall slender eucalyptus tree was placed to screen the house from the sun. "I planted other unkempt and wild things here," says Susan Crowell. "We designed the bronze-glass sunscreen to shade the interior and keep the winds from the glass in the living room area," Kappe explains.

Preceding pages: The house overlooks Naples Canal, which offers easy access by boat to Alamitos Bay and Santa Monica Bay.

BALBOA

PENINSULA

AND

CORONA

DEL

MAR

•

NEWPORT

BEACH

Traditional and vernacular styles abound in the residential community of Newport Beach. Yet in 1926 Rudolph Schindler broke the rules and gained the reputation of a maverick architect for his starkly modern Lovell Beach House. Architect Arthur Erickson and designer Barbara Barry continue the tradition of modern architecture in Newport with the recent design of a Balboa Peninsula house. Although the streamlined steel-and-glass pavilion pays less formal tribute to the works of Schindler than it does to the steel-I-beam-and-glass infill structures of Mies van der Rohe, or the glass block-and-steel Maison de Verre of Pierre Chareau, it is just as notable as a bold and consistent design.

"Commissioning an architect is a shot in the dark," says one of the residents. "We spent time telling Arthur Erickson, as well as our interior designer Barbara Barry, our feelings about living in a home and enjoying family life. We love having our family in the home, partaking in meals, cooking, serving, and entertaining. And Arthur and Barbara did it. They made a livable, casual beach house for our family."

"I suggested to my clients that it might be interesting to do something in white-painted steel and glass," explains Erickson. "Glass is basically sand, and it's watery. In fact, I suggested that they see the historic glass-block house, Maison de Verre, in Paris. They did, and we began to develop the house along those lines. The result is that their house is very beachy and aqua-colored from the glass."

"We placed the house to one side of the lot, rather than in the middle, and thus we got a more generous use and sense of the property," Erickson says, explaining his layout of the beach house. "Every room has a view of the beach."

The living room maintains the feeling of a wide-open, tranquil pavilion. The room offers a totally unobstructed view over a small reflecting pool to the dunes and the ocean. The master bath, designed by Erickson's partner, Francisco Kripacz, features a circular glass shower etched to provide privacy while allowing light to filter through the glass-block wall.

Creamy French limestone is used for the ground-level flooring inside and out, and visually unites the house with the beach. "The limestone is also used for walls that skirt one side of the property and form the base of the steel frame and glass block above," Erickson adds.

"Like the Maison de Verre, an upper deck to the master bedroom features a glass block floor."

Luckily, the first love of Barbara Barry's life is architecture, and she feels decoration works best when it marries the architecture. "I put on the architect's thinking cap and tried to think through Arthur's plans and extend his vision," says Barry. "My overall concept for the house was to honor the hierarchy of ocean, architecture, and decoration, and to try to make something that was seamless. The glass block is like an extension to the sky, and the French limestone is an extension of the sand. To maintain this atmosphere that Arthur set, I chose materials equal in strength to the glass and steel. They are all canvas-like—white, natural, and easy to care for, including white cotton sheeting, white linen, and white cotton slipcovers. In that quietness, nothing would interrupt."

"I don't feel the house is decorated," says the resident. "We wanted to use the colors of the ocean and sand—the limestone is like the sand, and the glass gives the color of the ocean."

Top: Seen against a glass-block wall, the curved, sandblasted glass staircase enclosure is a shimmering and elegant focal point in the living room. Wall, stair, and flooring are French limestone. The circular painting is by Tim Ebner.

Bottom: From the master bedroom—simply furnished with a maple bed and side table designed by Barbara Barry—the view through glass and glass block is layered and transparent. The room overlooks the courtyard.

Erickson's partner Francisco Kripacz designed the master bath with a capsule-shaped
stainless steel vanity, circular mirror, and circular glass shower enclosure.

Above: By moving the house to the side of the lot, a giant side courtyard, or outdoor room, as Erickson calls it, was created to bring in light and ocean views to each room and offer a place for outdoor dining. A gridded canopy shelters the space from direct sun.

Right: "A public walkway ran along one side of the lot," says Erickson. "Fortunately, it isn't heavily trafficked, and we walled the house off and set it above the path by three or four feet. We then planted the access with palms, and it now looks like part of the property."

JOE AND ETSUKO PRICE RESIDENCE, 1988

DESIGNED BY BART PRINCE

lived on a ranch where the nearest neighbor—my brother—was a mile away," explains Oklahoma-transplant Joe Price. "So coming out to any big city and being plunked in the middle of houses scared me to death. I specifically looked for land where I could eliminate neighbors. The Corona del Mar site is a small point, where we have neighbors five feet away on both sides, but architecturally we've blocked them out. The ocean becomes my prairie. This vast open space gives me the feeling of complete freedom and privacy just like we had back on the ranch."

Fitting the house to nature was the goal of Joe and Etsuko Price and their architect, Bart Prince. They believe in the principles of organic architecture espoused by Frank Lloyd Wright, and the house is not unlike his horizontal Prairie houses. The undulating, shingled, wood- and copper-sided Price House quite appropriately merges with its cliff-side setting. In fact, from the beach at Corona del Mar, their house can hardly be distinguished from the natural colors and forms of the cliff. And now that the torrey "five-finger" pine trees have grown up, it is nearly obscured from view.

Joe Price and his wife, Etsuko, gave the Asian Art Pavilion to the Los Angeles County Museum of Art. Their architect, Bart Prince, carried out its design according to the original plans by the late Bruce Goff, an Oklahoma architect who developed a unique style based on Wright's principles. Pieces from their Edo-period collection are also located in the tea-house on the ground level of the house, where scholars come to study the works. "I looked everywhere from Santa Barbara to La Jolla, and this was the nicest spot I could find within a reasonable distance of the museum," Price adds.

Inside the house is a complex set of spaces that interlock organically: a study and den for Joe Price, a children's wing with playroom and terrace for the couple's two daughters, a master bedroom suite, and a living-dining area. A large terrace is cantilevered off the living room and its form of interconnecting curves reflects the arrangement of the pods—rooms that extend from the central core of the house.

"The antique Japanese door that opens to my study is from Takayama, a very beautiful, historic Japanese town," says Etsuko Price. The wood spiral stair ascends from the courtyard to Joe Price's den. "The large roof of the main structure is made of solid wood members, laminated to each other to form an undulating wood roof visible from within," explains architect Bart Prince.

At one point the roof of undulating shingles extends to protect the children's terrace. "From without, this central portion of the structure is covered with wood shingles," says Bart Prince. "To differentiate what I call the pod units that radiate out from the structure, they are covered on the outside with standing-seam copper sheeting."

At the center of the house, a partially open-roofed courtyard with a swimming pool offers a view of the glu-laminated structure and access to all the major living spaces. On one side of this courtyard, a shingled wall and large stone gently hold in place what resembles a moon gate, the ceremonial entrance to Japanese gardens. Through this portal, a stone tunnel and path lead from the central courtyard to the teahouse on the ground level. There, the lawn is a shady, serene retreat open to the hillside garden and a path down to the beach. "I use the garden often, although I seldom go to the beach," says Joe Price. "Every evening I go out to my 'martini rock' to relax and watch the whales, porpoises, and seals."

Joe and Etsuko Price's house blends into the natural setting of trees, planting, and stones. They recently added the cliff-side garden, using both natural and fake stones. "The stones are *genuine* simulated stone," jokes Joe Price. "They are molds of real stones cast on location. Haruo Yamashiro, a Japanese gardener from Gardena, worked with us, and he won first prize for originality in the state for it," he adds.

Above: "The planting is all local species that can thrive in the saltwater setting," Etsuko explains about their cliff-side garden.

Left: At one point the organic roof of undulating shingles extends to protect the children's terrace. "From without, this central portion of the structure is covered with wood shingles," says architect Bart Prince. "To differentiate what I call the pod units that radiate out from the structure, they are covered on the outside with standing-seam copper sheeting."

Following pages: The curved wing of the house, at right, includes the teahouse on the ground level with Joe's den and terrace above.

Above: Joe's study and den contain contain conversation areas, a sunken media center, and a bar, and is one of the series of pods made of glu-laminated wood beams.

Left: Outside of Joe's den, a shaded terrace features a table and stools Frank Lloyd Wright designed for Price Tower, Wright's only skyscraper, which he created for Price's father in Bartlesville, Oklahoma.

Following pages: The garden courtyard with a swimming pool and small bridge is central to the house and displays its glu-laminated wood beam and shingled structure. Behind the circular window is the children's wing of the house; the suspended metal stair leads to their terrace.

MARTHA PADVE/SALLY AND DON MARTIN COTTAGE
CIRCA 1926–30

Natural rock formations at Crystal Cove inspired early residents to plant a few palm trees. In 1928, when the coast highway officially opened, the palm trees attracted tourists' attention and people came to live on the beach out-of-doors, in tents, or in one-room units built with canvas walls or thatched with palm fronds. It became known as a South Seas atoll, and its owners, James Irvine II and James Irvine III, who both enjoyed the cove, gave their friends permission to build small cottages set against the bluffs. The thatched twenties gave way to the more permanent wooden thirties. The foundations of the remaining Crystal Cove homes date back to those two periods, especially between 1924 and 1936. After the mid-1930s the Irvine Company assumed tighter control over its property and offered residents a leasing management arrangement or the opportunity to move their houses elsewhere. Since then, the Irvine Company has restricted any changes to the structures. Therefore, the community retains its appearance of the 1920s and 1930s, and the surrounding open land, used for cattle grazing, also recalls the landscape of the early California setting.

During its heyday, Crystal Cove's South Seas appearance attracted the silent film industry. For years, owners maintained the palm-thatch hut appearance to keep movie-makers happy. Among the numerous films made there are *Treasure Island* (1920 and 1934), *Storm Swept*

(1923) and *White Shadows of the South Seas* (1928).

Forty-six bungalow-style cottages with seventeen tiny coveted garages are located in this natural cove. The canyon narrows into Trancos Creek, which runs behind and east of the northern end of the district and divides it as it empties into the ocean at the southern end. Its roads are one car wide and most are dirt, though a few are paved with asphalt. The cottages are located at the base of the cliff along man-made roads. Palm fronds that thatched the original Crystal Cove huts can still be found on a few of them. The South Group is so-named because it is south of Trancos Creek but linked to the other cottages by a small wooden bridge. The vegetation adjacent to the bridge is lush with morning glory, bougainvillea, hibiscus, cup-of-gold, and a cluster of uncommon eucalyptus trees. It is an extraordinary site that also drew the Indians to settle long ago. A number of eighteenth-century Indian caves, called middens, were found one mile to the north in 1923. Recently, in front of the Padve/Martin house, the remains of a six-thousand-year-old civilization were discovered.

The gated community was unplanned; it developed naturally but is a unified neighborhood. Generations of the same families return here each summer or maintain the homes year-round. In 1980 when the community was designated a landmark, Crystal Cove boasted eight cottages of fourth generation and eleven cottages of third generation leaseholders. The land-mark process was aided by the recently-enacted Coastal Commission Act of 1976, which specified that "unique coastal communities should be enhanced and preserved." The present residents have a strong community feeling despite the fact that they lease their property.

Martha Padve has leased her bungalow in the South Group since the 1950s. "Lately I haven't the time to get to the house as often as I'd like, so I share it with friends Sally and Don Martin, who live here year-round," says Mrs. Padve.

"I love the concept of sharing. It suits the whole notion of this community," says Sally Martin. "Our current neighbors include a retired movie producer, an accountant, a judge, and a sculptress. We're all good friends who join in community parties, games, and events." The brown-shingled bungalow at the end of the cove was used in the filming of *Beaches,* starring Bette Midler. "*Creator* was filmed here, too," adds Don Martin. "And Peter O'Toole was friendly and fit right in with our small community."

Below: The Padve/Martin house is a bungalow with an addition at the back that steps up into the hillside. White trellis covers the pilings that hold up the large deck where the Martins entertain. The deck expands the small one-room living-dining-kitchen space. The next level up is occupied by the master bedroom, and farther up the hill is an open deck with a Jacuzzi.

Following pages: From the kitchen, Sally and Don Martin can see the sunset, and while cooking, they can converse with guests across the tiled counter to the living room area.

Top: The master bedroom is reached by an outdoor stair. To take full advantage of the continuous band of bungalow windows, the bed is raised, and a mirrored wall doubles the ocean view.

Bottom: The Martins enjoy most of their meals out-of-doors on the terrace where light-colored striped cushions set a sunny tone.

Right: Simple board-and-batten walls, exposed ceiling beams, and wood floors reveal the humble beach-cottage roots of the house. A mirrored wall behind the inlaid wood desk expands a corner of the living room. Built against the hill, a guest bedroom is located beyond the mirrored wall.

MOSS POINT HOUSE

MICHAEL AND LINDA HALL RESIDENCE, 1917

INTERIORS DESIGNED BY LINDA HALL

Gables silhouetted against the sky and a picket fence with an arbor gate are the first glimpses one receives of the picture-perfect Moss Point House, which is hidden from view by gardens and landscaping. This New England–style beach house with cream-colored shingles and powder blue shutters and trim was built in 1917 as the summer residence of Colonel Henry House, former Secretary of State under Woodrow Wilson. Locally referred to as Moss Point House, it has been called alternatively the western White House and the Woodrow Wilson House because President Wilson came out to visit the Colonel in 1919 when he was seeking support for the League of Nations.

The two-acre site is located on one of the most gentle, beautiful promontories in the area. "It's a house that has been shielded from public view. You have to be on the property or on the water to see it. It's not highly visible from any street, and that's part of its charm—that it's tucked away," explains the resident, interior designer Linda Hall.

The house is actually three stories high and has twenty rooms, but it appears smaller because it is set into the hill. Altogether the two-acre site owned by Constance Morthland

includes a tennis court, volleyball court, swimming pool, and meandering flagstone pathways through flower gardens and eucalyptus, star, and Monterey pine trees.

"I've lived on the beach my whole life," adds Dr. Michael Hall. "And Linda and I have lived in the area since 1970. We owned a house two houses south, but when the opportunity came in 1985 to move here we took advantage of it." Constance Morthland—who has lived in an adjacent Federal-style residence since the 1920s—purchased Moss Point House in the 1980s to ensure its preservation. She has leased it to Dr. and Mrs. Hall since that time.

"We decorated the house with the express purpose of keeping it as close as possible in feeling to the period," explains Linda Hall. "Some of the pieces are older than the house, but they are representative of things that could have been in the house at the time it was built." One of the most pleasant spaces in Moss Point House is the dining room, which resembles a greenhouse perched amid the trees, where two broad corner windows open to views of the lush landscaping and the cove beach west of the house.

"It's very hard to maintain the style of the house in the elements at the beach, so that some furnishings don't totally fall apart," she adds. "You have to use available modern-day products and try to blend them in an old and traditional vein."

The best feature of the house is the L-shaped porch, which includes both open and closed spaces: one roofed area that wraps around from the side porch that displays antique wicker, and one open-roof side with glass walls that shield the wind but allow outdoor dining under the sun and moon. A nautical blue umbrella provides shade, and contemporary outdoor furniture is covered with gray-and-white striped cushions.

Brick and flagstone paths wind down from the porches to a sunning platform and two observation points. Below are the cove beaches and tide pools where the Chinese cook employed by Colonel House's daughter, Minnie Davis, used to spearfish for dinner.

"What I like best about the house is that you enter another time zone," says Linda Hall. "Sitting out on that porch or being inside the house takes you out of the twentieth century."

Below: The side entrance to the house—through the picket fence and arbor gate to the side porch and a side door entrance—is informal. "Porches are rare these days, and that's my favorite room," resident Linda Hall says.

Following pages: A wood-railed porch wraps around two sides of the gable-roofed, shingled house, providing views to the south and west.

Top: One of two octagonal observation points on the property is set over the cliffs of Moss Point.

Bottom: At the crest of Moss Point on the sprawling lawn in front of the house, a red tile–paved platform provides space for sunbathing.

Right: For many years Minnie B. Davis, Colonel House's daughter, spent her summers at Moss Point House. Landscape architect Fred Lang would rejuvenate the grounds each spring before her return, covering the banks with poor-man's weatherglass, which was specially grown for Mrs. Davis at a local nursery.

Gables, a picket fence, and an arbor gate are the first glimpses one receives of Moss Point House. This New England–style beach house was built in 1917 as the summer residence of Colonel Henry House, former Secretary of State under Woodrow Wilson.

Architecturally formal and yet surrounded by fragrant, overgrown, informal gardens, this extraordinary South Laguna villa dominates its point setting. It blends Italianate and French architectural elements indiscriminately but confidently, much like a vernacular structure, without conscious pretensions of aspiring purely to either culture.

"For the interiors, the resident asked that every room be different, to capture a different style and be a kind of 'Disneyland' of rooms," explains David A. Harte, who designed the interiors and collaborated on the gardens for the resident, an international businessman. "He wanted a warm country kitchen and a formal French living room or salon. Throughout the house we used imported French and English antiques and European fabrics." Fine furnishings from numerous other countries are found here as well. In the living room are a gilded circular card table and chairs from a Russian palace and, in a far corner, a covered Meissen jardiniere is displayed on a gilded Italian pedestal.

An elegant, curved stair draws attention upwards from the spacious entrance area, which is finished in limestone and white Carrara and black Absolute marbles. "The gold-leaf stair bannister has a leaf motif in the center of each bronze rondel," explains Harte. "It came from the Carnegie Mansion, now the Cooper-Hewitt Museum in New York."

Though the house is large, it comprises interior and exterior rooms of intimate scale. Since the swimming pool is indoors with a swim-up-to bar, the main oceanfront terrace is a small outdoor room created for the formal parterre-shaped Jacuzzi. "The pool shells came from Indonesia," explains Flores. French doors lead to an informal den and a guest bedroom, and the balconies above open to the formal living room and music room, and the master bedroom on the upper level.

The terrace is defined on the edge of the cliff by a domed gazebo—the sole remains of the original Charlie Chaplin estate which once stood on the property. Although Chaplin never owned the property, his name was attached to the former estate because of his occasional use of it. "The gazebo was in such ruin that it had to be completely rebuilt," says Harte, "but it was beautifully sited and worked well with our design."

"We wanted a full-grown, casual feeling with every color of the spectrum," landscape designer Ruben Flores says of his collaboration with Harte. "And we wanted the formality of the walk but with an abundant feeling of plants that have overgrown their areas. Many perennials were used, so flowers bloom almost year-round, and every pot on the property has bulbs."

Flores worked with Harte to capture a year-round vision of the gardens of southern France. "Above the gazebo are four different bougainvillea and climbing roses all mixed together," he explains. "Roses are around the perimeter, and a thousand freesia are planted in this area. Impatiens fill the borders during the summertime and, during the winter, there are pansies."

"We feel that the house is the showplace of the Pacific," Harte says proudly, "because it's unique for its gardens on this cliff-side, oceanfront setting and its concept of a home with rooms for any mood."

The front of the house is first seen at an angle from the entrance gazebo. Although the facade is designed formally and symmetrically, the overall feeling is that of coming in through a side garden gate, which emphasizes the landscape and the oceanside setting. A triple layer of tiles at the roof eaves and upper window frame creates a quaint and picturesque detail.

Top: "The residents asked for a formal French living room," recalls interior designer David A. Harte. Gilded ceiling molding was handcrafted and the cream- and gold-fringed draperies and valances carry out the same formal yet warm color scheme.

Bottom: The master bedroom enjoys views of the sunsets from a large, partially-covered balcony.

Left: Surrounded by baskets, shells, and jardinieres that overflow with blossoming plants, the Jacuzzi occupies the main terrace.

Following pages: "The entrance gazebo was inspired by one I had seen in London," Harte explains. A low rail with classical balusters defines a formal space, the center of which is crowned by the metal-and-wire gazebo frame.

Top: The gilded, 1880s peacock bed from India is the tour de force of the master bedroom. Beside it are French 1880s marble-top commodes that hold dolphin lamps made from 1870s English architectural details.

Bottom: A shell-framed mirror made by a Laguna artist is placed above the circa 1875 French double sink in the provincial-style guest house.

Right: The staircase in the main house was originally in the Carnegie Mansion in New York.

ACKNOWLEDGEMENTS

Melba Levick and Elizabeth McMillian wish to thank the residents who graciously opened their beach houses and the architects and designers who gave their time and support: Lynn and Stanley Byer, John Lautner, Annette Smith, Wayne Williams, David Anawalt, Charles Moore, John Ruble and Buzz Yudell, Charles Arnoldi and Katie Anawalt, Olivia Newton-John and Matt Lattanzi, Chris Lattanzi, Sue Steinberg, James and Nancy Chuda, Saundra Abbott, Erin Ferrucci, Ilene and Stanley Gold, Ron Goldman and Bob Firth, Dan and Kristi Stevens, Lisette and Norman Ackerburg, Richard Meier, Karen and David Gray, John Cottrell, Romy and Neal Israel, Steven Ehrlich, Lyn and Bill Norton, Frank Gehry, Carol and Roy Doumani, Robert Graham, Paul and Janice Shank, Andrea Rich, Frank Israel, Katina Torino, Frank Burton Wilson, Richard Huddleson, Ronald and Susan Crowell, Ray and Shelley Kappe, Arthur Erickson, Barbara Barry, Joe and Etsuko Price, Bart Prince, Martha Padve, Sally and Don Martin, Constance Morthland, Michael and Linda Hall, David A. Harte, and Ruben Flores; and a special thanks to Jerry Lomax, Linda Otto and Allan Landsburg, and Ed Niles.